MW01295770

Into the Heart of SoulCollage®

The images on the cover of this book represent a SoulCollage® card in my deck. I call it "Diving In." Here is what this card said to me in my journal:

I Am the One Who is free-form diving into the many-colored flowering heart. I Am the One Who is almost completely immersed in the heart. I Am the One Who sees within the heart all the many rainbow-colored bits and pieces of my life. I Am the One Who gives image to these pieces with SoulCollage®.

I Am the One Who feels safe diving into the heart of SoulCollage® because I know that the hands of Spirit are holding the process, and as They hold the process, They hold me. The hands safely contain all my inner work so that I feel protected as I dive right in.

My gift to you is the courage to dive into the heart of life, the heart of your soul, the heart of the SoulCollage® process. I give you the freedom to make this dive. I give you trust that all is well.

My message for you today is this: Enjoy the moment as you dive into the flowering heart that is your life. Savor the movement as well as the stillness as you safely journey within.

Into the Heart of SoulCollage®

Diving Into the Many Gifts and Possibilities of SoulCollage®

Anne Marie Bennett

87 Creative and Inspiring Essays That Explore
Creativity
Committee Suit
Shadow
Council Suit
Seasons and Holidays
Lessons from Television
Difficult Times
The Big Picture of SoulCollage®

Copyright 2016 Anne Marie Bennett
All rights reserved.

ISBN: 1519798776
ISBN 13: 9781519798770
Library of Congress Control Number: 2015920859
CreateSpace Independent Publishing Platform
North Charleston, South Carolina

Images on cover collage purchased on Dreamstime.com
©lenchik ©Nikkizalewski ©Christinlola

Dedicated to all of our
KaleidoSoul Kindred Spirits
around the world.

You know who you are!

Without your presence,
this book would not have been
called into existence.

Permission is granted by Hanford Mead Publishers, Inc. for use of quotations from *SoulCollage® Evolving* (2010) by Seena B. Frost.

The author offers thanks to Karen Mann, Stephanie Pacheco, and Glenda Cedarleaf, for allowing me to use their quotes, photos, and guided imagery within the context of this book.

Praise for Anne Marie Bennett's
Through the Eyes of SoulCollage®:
Reflections on Life Via the SoulCollage® Lens
Now available on Amazon

Dip into this collection of Anne Marie's life stories, and you will discover many ideas for your own personal SoulCollage® deck. She describes how very different Neters came to live among her cards, and you will be surprised and charmed. You might just be nudged to search for images to create new cards for your own deck! This book will help you discover the wisdom hidden in your own imagination.

~ Seena B. Frost, Founder of SoulCollage® and author of *SoulCollage® Evolving*

This book is not just for those who do SoulCollage® - it's for everyone who is looking for something to lift them up. I couldn't turn the pages fast enough when my copy arrived in the mail - I even had to take it in the bathtub with me when I soaked one night because I just had to keep reading! I speak from the heart of how much this book touched me - and will continue to touch me for a long time to come.

~ Barbara, SoulCollage® Facilitator in Wisconsin, author of *Through Frankie's Eyes*

Just got mine on Wednesday. Can't put it down. I take it everywhere with me like a good friend and have already tried several of the suggestions. I opened randomly and it came to Lesson 55 on Grounding. Just what I needed to read about. Now I am going back to the beginning!

~ Linda, SoulCollager in Massachusetts

Loving this book! Anne Marie's insights into life and the present moments are wonderfully written and humbling. A good reminder to put our technology down and remember to enjoy life and the simple moments.

~ Denyse, SoulCollage® Facilitator in Connecticut

I read the book from cover to cover and later will follow many of the suggestions given for making and working with my cards. I absolutely loved this book and it'll be a foundation for me as a SoulCollage® Facilitator for many years to come.

~ Linda, SoulCollage® Facilitator in Florida

I am just in the very beginning of my SoulCollage® journey and was fortunate enough to take an online class with Anne Marie. This book has deepened my understanding of this amazing process and I can't say enough about how rich the material is.

~ Fay, SoulCollager in Massachusetts

You have done a beautiful job of taking us by the hand and then guiding us to whatever is next for us. I love that you give us permission to open the book wherever it lands for us. I just read the first three chapters and feel so taken care of! Like you tucked me in with a warm cuddly blanket . . . each chapter thus far has touched on many primary concerns and experiences that I have had myself. Thank you!

~ SoulCollage® Facilitator Cheryl in Illinois

Table of Contents

Introduction · xi
Vocabulary · xiii
How to Use This Book · xv
Suggestions for Facilitators · xvii

The Essays:
Creativity ·1
Committee Suit · 11
Shadow · 53
Council Suit · 91
Seasons and Holidays · 115
Everything I Need to Know About Life I Learned from Television · 145
Difficult Times · 175
SoulCollage®: The Big Picture · 205

Acknowledgements · 253
Resources · 255

Introduction

I AM SITTING in my Quiet Room right now, pondering what I will say in the Introduction to this second book of essays about the SoulCollage® process. Typewritten pages of the manuscript are scattered around my desk, a spicy pine-scented candle glows beside me, *Sanctuary of Peace* by Thaddeus is softly echoing in the background . . . and my heart is full.

This past year I have been on a wondrous journey as I compiled the 174 essays that you will find in *Through the Eyes of SoulCollage®* as well as this book, *Into the Heart of SoulCollage®.* I have seen the heart of my own life's journey more clearly and from a broader perspective through these essays and I hope that you will be inspired to look at your own journey with new eyes and transformed heart as well. SoulCollage® gives us the gift of being able to view all the pieces of our lives with acceptance and compassion. I hope that you are able to open to receive this gift as you read and experience these stories with me.

The essays in this volume focus on the Committee Suit of inner voices, the Council Suit of archetypes, and the concept of integrating parts of us that are out of balance. Other essays center on how to use SoulCollage® when our lives become turbulent or during the earth's changing seasons. I have also included essays about creativity and self-expression as well as the bigger picture of SoulCollage®. And finally, some of the stories here are about the lessons we can learn by staying open when watching television!

In 2016 we celebrate the 10th anniversary of our KaleidoSoul Kindred Spirits membership, so it is fitting that this volume of essays is published now. I am looking back on 10 years of SoulCollagers who embraced our mission of bringing like-minded creatives together to immerse ourselves in the process of SoulCollage®. 10 years of our weekly member newsletter, *Soul Treasures*. 10 years of monthly tele-classes about SoulCollage®. 10 years of inspiring, creative community. 10 years of diving into our own hearts and lives by learning more about ourselves through the process of SoulCollage®!

I find it interesting that I am writing the Introduction to this book at the very end of the writing process. But perhaps it is fitting, as it invites me to look at the stories here as a whole, and reminds me of why I wrote all of them in the first place: to share the gift of SoulCollage® with those who are thirsty for wholeness and hungering for positive transformation and self-compassion.

May you, dear reader, be touched by these essays about SoulCollage® and the stories from my own life that I use to illustrate them. May you be gently guided to dive fearlessly into your own heart's story. May the process of SoulCollage® guide and bless you; may it keep you safe on all of your own inner explorations. May your own heart be full.

Anne Marie Bennett
Beverly, MA
January 2016

Vocabulary

HERE ARE SOME words I use throughout the book and my own short definitions of them, as informed by Seena Frost in her book *SoulCollage® Evolving*:

Archetypes: These are themes or motifs that play out over our individual lives.

✓ *12 step reference*

Committee Suit: These are cards that we make to represent our inner voices or personality parts.

Community Suit: These are cards that we make to represent family, friends, teachers, pets and those sentient beings whose lives have touched our own. My book *Through the Eyes of SoulCollage®* has more information about this suit.

Companions: These are cards we make to honor the energetic dimensions of our lives, including animal guides and our body's seven chakra centers. My book *Through the Eyes of SoulCollage®* has more information about this suit.

✓ *Sponser*

Council Suit: These are cards that we make to represent archetypal energies that have touched our lives.

Deck: This is a set of SoulCollage® cards that represent different parts of one's life journey. It includes the above suits as well as cards that symbolize The One. There is no prescribed number of cards in a SoulCollage® deck.

Neter: We refer to each card, or energy, in our decks as a Neter, which is an ancient Egyptian word that meant "The One" as well as "The Many." We use it to refer to an energy or figure in our deck that acts as an ally, guide, or challenger in our lives.

Suit: A SoulCollage® deck often consists of four suits or categories that represent a different part of our life. The four suits as introduced by SoulCollage® Founder Seena B. Frost are: Committee, Community, Companions, and Council.

The One: You can choose to call "The One" from which all else springs by any name that appeals to you. Some people call it Source; others call it The Divine, Spirit, God, or Allah.

use a sc card as a source for my paintings

The Many: This is the term we use for all the manifest parts and pieces of our lives, as represented by all our cards in the four suits.

My Moon Mothers
My Star Child/ren

How to Use This Book

Time for Reflection

At the end of each essay, I've offered some suggestions for how you can relate my story to your own life and your own work with SoulCollage®. There are card making ideas, journaling ideas, and lots of other creative ideas too! Feel free to use these or adapt them for your own personal use.

SoulCollage® Examples

In some of my stories, I describe one of my own SoulCollage® cards. At the end of each of these particular essays you will find a link to a page on my website where you can take a peek at this card. Please be aware that each of these pages is password protected, so be sure to note the password given before opening the web page.

SoulCollage® does not advocate copying or infringing on the copyrighted works of others in any way. SoulCollage® cards are made for personal use. Part of personal use is sharing. When I share my personal stories, I also want to share my cards with you.

SoulCollage® Resources

Once in a while, I have added a resource for your reference. I hope you find these recommended books and websites helpful.

If You Are New to SoulCollage®

1. Start at the beginning with the first essay. Read one every couple of days, and at the same time, read Seena B. Frost's book *SoulCollage® Evolving*, or some of the content pages at KaleidoSoul.com.

2. Skim through the *Table of Contents* and *Vocabulary* listings at the beginning of this book. Listen inside yourself for what most intrigues you and start with *that* section first. You might want to read a few essays within that topic and let your reading inspire you to make some cards.

3. After you've made some cards based on the suggestions in the Time for Reflection offered after each essay, try out some of the ideas in the last section, *Using Your SoulCollage® Cards.*

If You Have Experience with SoulCollage®

1. Start at the beginning. Read one essay per week and spend some quality time with the "Time for Reflection" section at the end.

2. Choose the section that you're most curious about and start there instead of at the beginning.

3. Open the book at random and read whatever essay you land on. Take it to heart. Do the "Time for Reflection" exercises at the end, or make up your own!

Suggestions for Facilitators

I DIDN'T WRITE these essays with SoulCollage® Facilitators in mind, but I've had many Facilitators tell me that they've been inspired to create workshops based on what they've read. With that in mind, here are some ways to use this book if you are a SoulCollage® Facilitator.

1. Choose a topic that you're not completely comfortable explaining to others. Start with that section. Read the essays and do the "Time for Reflection" exercises for yourself until you feel more comfortable with this topic.

2. Start at the beginning and read each essay until you come to one that stirs you up inside. You'll notice your creative juices starting to flow! Create a workshop theme that revolves around the topic of this essay. Use the "Time for Reflection" activities or journaling questions to share with your workshop participants. Create your own SoulCollage® card or cards on this topic to share as well.

3. Give each person in your monthly group a copy of this book. Invite each person to share their favorite essay at your next gathering, as well as a SoulCollage® card they were inspired to create as a result of it.

4. Read aloud one of the essays to your workshop participants. Invite them to discuss the topic in dyads, small groups, or the large group. Allow time for card making afterwards.

5. If you are not yet a trained Facilitator, go to SoulCollage.com/facilitator-training for more information about locations and content of Facilitator Trainings around the world.

Creativity

Overview

Many people are drawn to the process of SoulCollage® because they are inherently creative. Even if you don't describe yourself as "creative" or "artistic," chances are there's a part of you who longs to bring this creative voice out of the shadows.

One of the beautiful things about SoulCollage® is that it meets each of us right where we are, no questions asked. It's a simple enough process that anyone can do. Magazine images, scissors and glue - that's all you need to get started. The creativity will follow naturally as you trust your inner guidance.

CHAPTER 1

We Are All Artists

I FIND MANY people in my workshops who are drawn to SoulCollage® because they can't draw and therefore don't consider themselves "artists." It was the same for me at the beginning. I had been artistic and creative all my life, but I never would have used the word "artist" to describe myself.

My father could draw a cat, a person, a diagram of a room (anything, really), and it would be instantly recognizable and "good." I did not inherit his talent for drawing realistic images so I believed that I wasn't "good enough" to be an artist.

In my workshops over the years, I've seen thousands of SoulCollage® cards. Sometimes we get excited over how one card is so "beautiful" or "powerful" or "amazing." But a card is still "beautiful art" even if the majority of people wouldn't label it like that.

I tell everyone who does SoulCollage® with me (with apologies to Will Rogers): *I never met a SoulCollage® card I didn't like.* As long as the card has moved the artist a little further on the journey inward, then it can be called "good art," and only then can it be called beautiful.

I now can irrevocably say, "I am an artist," so I created an inner artist card (see link below) to remind me of this. Art isn't just about perspective and detail and form and negative space. It's about going deeply within and expressing that depth with color, with image, with collage, with every fiber of our being. Every SoulCollage® card (and I mean *every single one*) is a true piece of art, and the goodness of that art is all about how it touches us inside, at our core.

3

Time for Reflection

Do you have a SoulCollage® card for the part of you who is an artist, regardless of the fact that you can or cannot draw? If not, start collecting images so you can make one.

Try saying these words out loud to yourself this week in a loving, gentle way: *I am an artist.*

What inner parts of you get in the way of calling yourself an artist? Maybe one of those voices needs to be honored with a SoulCollage® card this week too.

SoulCollage® Example

Please visit KaleidoSoul.com/into-the-heart-creativity
The password for this page is: artist

The topic to scroll down to is:
Artist

CHAPTER 2

Art That Fits Just Right

Art should be something like a good armchair in which
to rest from physical fatigue.

~ HENRI MATISSE

MY HUSBAND BOUGHT a recliner several years ago. He tried it out in the
store, chose a color that went with our bedroom decor, and had it delivered. I loved his enthusiasm for this chair, but whenever *I* sat in it, I
couldn't seem to get comfortable. It turns out it suited him perfectly
because he has short legs and a long torso, but my body is the opposite.

I kept this in mind when I was shopping for an easy chair for my
study a while back. I made sure not only to look at colors, fabrics, and
price, but how it felt when I sat in it. Believe me, I sat in quite a few
before I found the right one! I knew immediately that it "fit" my body
because as soon as I sank into it and pushed back into reclining mode,
my body and mind echoed the same chorus: "Ahhhh, yes!"

According to Matisse, I should look at my art in the same way. There
are so many modes of artistic self-expression, so many paths of creativity to
choose from. Pottery, sculpting, scrapbooking, altered books, beadwork,
jewelry making, altered art, rubber stamping, watercolors, oil painting,
knitting, furniture refinishing, crayons, chalks, gardening, cooking, collage . . . The list goes on and on. It is my job as an artist to fit my artwork
to my inner and outer needs at any given moment. It is my responsibility
to find a manner of self-expression that "fits" me just right.

Time for Reflection

Which kinds of creativity serve you with physical, emotional, and spiritual rest?

How can you incorporate more of this type of art into your life?

Is there an art form you are using that doesn't serve you in this way? In what way is it serving you instead? Do you need to continue with this art form or can you let it go?

Do you have a SoulCollage® card for the part of you who is an artist? If so, journal with it. If not, create one!

CHAPTER 3

Throw That Paint!

Life is a great big canvas, and you should throw all the
paint on it that you can.

~ DANNY KAYE

I GREW UP in the 50's and 60's with parents who had survived the Great
Depression, so my early years consisted of one lesson after another about
scarcity. We may have had a drawer full of beautiful candles in the din-
ing room, but we never lit them because one day the electricity might
go out. There were shelves of canned goods in the basement, but we
weren't allowed to eat them because we might need them one day in case
of an emergency.

Today I can understand intellectually that these lessons in scarcity
were necessary because of what my parents had been through. But it's
taken me many years to begin to learn the lessons of abundance instead.

This is why I love creating collage! It feeds my sense of abundance
and of having more-than-enough. I thoroughly enjoy digging through
all of my art supplies, embellishments and images, to find just the right
ones to add to my work in progress.

But it's not just about art. Perhaps you don't consider yourself an
"artist." That's okay! The quotation above gives us a message about
how to live life in a big, joyful, wide, colorful, abundant manner. Maybe
you're not throwing paint on an art canvas, but you can certainly throw
a whole lot of love, joy, and gratitude onto the canvas that is your life.

Time for Reflection

If you like creating art, spend a few hours this month playing around with your art supplies in a big way. Use a lot of paint. Use it all! Make a much bigger creation than you usually create. Only use your favorite colors, and make this joyful creation *just for you.* Don't save anything for later!

Spend some time pondering how you can broaden, expand, and make your life bigger. Discover how you can really live into all the tastes, sounds, smells, sights, and textures of your world. "Bigger" means that you realize you have more space inside you for gratitude, love, and joy.

Spend some time focusing on the concepts of scarcity and abundance. When and where have each showed up in your life so far? Create some SoulCollage® cards for your deck around these themes.

CHAPTER 4

The Self-Expression Express

WHEN I WAS 15, I had a fun job in a library. I have always loved books so I really loved this job. A few other kids my age worked there with me. During break times, we would be in the conference room together. They'd be chatting, and I'd be scribbling happily in my journal. Sometimes I'd join in their conversations, but mainly I used my free time for writing.

One day, Bob (one of my peers) challenged me. "Why are you always writing in that notebook?" There was only curiosity in his voice. At first I was startled; then confusion took over! I had *no idea* why I wrote so much. I just did. One of the older librarians was having lunch with us that day, and she overheard Bob's question. She saw how puzzled I was and noticed my inability to answer, so she responded for me. "Anne Marie writes to express herself," she said.

Aha! A lot of puzzle pieces fell into place right then, and my eyes shone with the absolute truth that her words gave me. *Yes, that's exactly it*, I thought with gladness. Writing is *my* means of self-expression.

The writing is mine. Mine alone. It got me through a difficult adolescence, and many a confusing love gone wrong. It got me through my challenging college years, and through my first teaching job 500 miles from everyone and everything I knew. It got me through a difficult decade with my stepfamily, and it got me through two cancer diagnoses. It is still getting me through. It is one of the few things in my life that has been a constant, positive companion since I was very young.

When I discovered SoulCollage® in 2005, my writing became deeper and fed my soul even more. I now count SoulCollage® right up there with writing as my main mode for self-expression.

Time for Reflection

What is the one thing in your life that is yours alone, your main mode of self-expression? It doesn't have to be a solitary pursuit like my writing. It could be cooking, dancing, gardening, jewelry making, teaching, singing or something else that is uniquely yours.

What is something you can do today to activate and celebrate this one thing?

Committee Suit

Overview

The Committee Suit represents what Seena Frost, the founder of SoulCollage®, calls the psychological dimension of our lives. You can also think of it as your *inner world*: all those inner voices inside of you that you hear chatting away, no matter what happens in your life. You might want to refer to them as "parts" or "characters." I know someone who refers to these parts as her "inner tribe." Another popular reference is "inner family." You can call your inner committee anything you want! The important thing to remember is that they belong to *you*.

The other suits deepen our sense of the "real," outer world (Community Suit) and the mystical, sometimes unseen world (Companions Suit, Council Suit). The Committee Suit is the only suit that focuses on what is going on *inside* of us. This brings a sense of wholeness to our lives and to our SoulCollage® decks as well.

More information about the Committee Suit can be found here: KaleidoSoul.com/innervoices

CHAPTER 5

Who's Driving Your Bus Today?

I LIKE TO think of my inner Committee members as riding in a jaunty old school bus, painted with a myriad of swirly bright colors.

On an ideal day, my authentic self is driving the bus. This is the part of me who is my deepest, truest self. It is the channel that Spirit uses to speak to and through me. This authentic self is the energy within that loves and unconditionally accepts *all* of my many parts.

When I get overwhelmed or caught up in behavior that is getting in the way of my ability to love myself (e.g., overeating, nagging at my husband, berating myself . . . etc.), then I know that someone other than my authentic self has grabbed the wheel of the bus and is driving.

But guess what? The more I practice SoulCollage®, the more I am able to differentiate the various parts of me who occupy my inner rainbow-colored bus. And the better I get to know them, the easier it is to notice when one of them takes over the "steering wheel" of my life. It is also easier to find out why they have hijacked my inner family's vehicle, and then to accompany them back to their rightful seat (which is never the driver's seat).

Time for Reflection

Take several index cards and write the following on each one in a bright-colored marker: **Who is driving my bus today?**

Put each card somewhere prominent where you'll see it and be reminded to ask yourself this question often.

See if you can notice the subtle shift that occurs when one of your inner Committee members takes over the "driver's seat" of your life.

CHAPTER 6

Terms of Endearment

WHEN I WAS first learning about SoulCollage®, I became vividly aware of all the thoughts that were going on in my mind at any given point of my day. My inner Committee constantly had things to say to me. This self-talk was ongoing, even in my dreams. *Wait! Don't go there, go here instead. Are you really going to wear THAT???? You're tired now . . . better stop. Slow down and listen to what he is saying; it's important. Buy the melon instead of the candy bars. That color doesn't look very good on you.*

As you also may have experienced, sometimes other Neters actually answer back, bringing out inner conversations of the finest (or sometimes headachy) kind.

During the time that these inner conversations were first flooding into my awareness, I read somewhere a suggestion about using a "pet name" when we talk to ourselves. This is the kind of endearment we use when we're talking to a loved one: *sweetie, honey, huggy-bear, sweet pea, darlin'* . . . etc.

At the time, the theatre where I worked was mounting a brilliant production of *Kiss of the Spider Woman*, which I was privileged to see numerous times. One song in particular has stayed in my mind and heart all these years. It's called *Dear One*, and four actors sing it to each other from the four corners of the stage: a mother with her son, and two young lovers.

So I began using Dear One as my own personal pet name when the inner Committee voices got a little out of hand. It's amazing how much of a difference it makes to be hearing the above self-talk comments with a dash of Dear One thrown in: *Dear One, let's go do this today instead of that.*

You're tired now, Dear One, let's rest for a bit. Dear One, I think we'd better listen to what this teacher is saying. Let's buy some fruit today instead of candy bars, Dear One.

If you stop and think about it, you probably use terms of endearment like this all the time with your cat, your dog, your children, grandchildren, partner, friends, and other loved ones. Why not use a loving pet name with your own beautiful self? It will make all the difference!

Time for Reflection

Spend a week becoming aware of the pet names that you call your loved ones. Did a parent or grandparent call you something special when you were little? Pay attention to pet names that are used on TV shows that you enjoy or books that you're reading. Make a list.

Choose your own personal "term of endearment" and use it often with yourself. Print it out on a large sheet of paper and hang it where you'll see it often. It may take a while to discover just the "right" one, so be patient.

Make a SoulCollage® card that gives image to this special name.

CHAPTER 7

Silly and Blessed

A FEW YEARS ago I was on a personal retreat at Kripalu in western Massachusetts. I was sitting on a comfy couch in the spacious lobby on a quiet morning, gazing out over the Berkshire Mountains. It was peaceful and I was seriously intent on the book I was beginning to read.

After several minutes, a young couple settled on a sofa several feet away from me. They were newly in love; I could tell because of the way they were whispering and giggling together. They went on like this for several minutes, at some points bursting into loud, joyful laughter. Listening to them made me smile inside. I thought of how long it had been since *I* had taken time to simply sit and laugh like that (with or without someone special beside me).

Instead of wishing they would go away, I closed my eyes and basked in their unabashed silliness. It seemed to wash me clean of my own inner seriousness, which had been prominent that morning.

Later that day, the book I was reading indicated that the word "silly" comes from the Gaelic word for "blessed." Aha! A new revelation! I did indeed feel blessed by being so near to that couple's silliness. It was downright contagious.

I made a Sense of Humor card for my deck a long time ago (see link below), but I didn't know that's what I was making at the time. I just knew I loved the images and they seemed to belong together. When I let them "speak" to me, they seemed to be reminding me of my own abundant sense of humor, my own ability to be silly, to laugh at myself.

Now that I stop to think about it, I realize that I don't give this Neter enough latitude in my life. I do love to laugh. I'm witty and I take great delight in making others laugh. But my inner Committee part who is *serious* usually has lots more power in my life. In making this card, I have shifted the balance inside of me.

Time for Reflection

Find some time this week to do something completely silly. Notice if this action blesses you in some way.

Make a SoulCollage® card to honor your own inner "Silly One" or a card for your "Sense of Humor."

Perhaps there's a comedian or comic actor in your life who has enriched your world with laughter. If so, create a SoulCollage® Community card for him or her.

Think and journal about times when laughter made a difference in your life. Make a list of books, movies, or TV shows that make you laugh. Be sure to *read, listen to,* or *watch* at least one of these every week. *Notice the difference.*

SoulCollage® Example

Please visit KaleidoSoul.com/into-the-heart-committee
The password for this page is: self

The topic to scroll down to is:
Sense of Humor

CHAPTER 8

All My Children

I ONCE HEARD Seena Frost say that she regularly asks herself this question: *Have I been faithful to my child today?* She is referring to her "inner child" of course, not one of her biological offspring. Seena also recommends that every SoulCollager create a Committee card for their Happy Child. I made a Happy Child card right away, and as I continued with my SoulCollage® practice, I found myself creating several different cards for my own Inner Child. After hearing Seena suggest that we give names to our cards, I decided to call my Inner Child Julianna which is the name of my favorite childhood doll.

Seena also encourages us to separate out the various childlike energies onto individual cards. This inspired me to notice the varying energies and emotions of my inner child and to create cards for each of them. My deck now contains cards to honor my inner Happy Child, Creative Child, Playful Child, and Mystical Child.

I also did inner work over the course of a few years that involved some shadowed aspects of my inner child, and out of that work came cards that reflected my Rebellious Child, my Lonely Child, and my Shamed Child.

When I was growing up, showing emotions other than happiness and gratitude were just not acceptable. So it was a healing and affirming process to honor each aspect, each face, each feeling of my Inner Child with its own beautiful card. My Rebellious Child, when young, was never given space to be angry. My Lonely Child was often tucked into bed with no one to wipe away her tears. My Shamed Child was brought up with the feeling of "not enough." Giving each of them image and voice through the SoulCollage® process has given them (and consequently, me) the emotional acceptance that I never experienced as a child.

Along the way, I also created a card with an image of myself at 12 years old, surrounded by divine beings. I've come to believe that these divine beings were with me, even when my childhood took an abusive and difficult turn. Having that particular card in my deck now is a beautiful reminder that I was (and am) never alone. I also made a card called Mommy and Me, which represents how my Inner Child now feels about having an Inner Mother who accepts her exactly as she is.

As you can see, sometimes creating a series of cards for your deck turns into its own journey! I hope that you will find inspiration in my tribe of Inner Children, and that you will find your own unique ways to be faithful to *your* Inner Child.

Time for Reflection

Journal with this question: *How have I been faithful to my inner child lately?*

Do you have a card for your Happy Child? If not, set an intention to find some images and create one. If you do have one, set it on your desk or nightstand where you will see it often. Make time to do some journaling with your Happy Child. What does she/he need from you this week?

Flip through some magazines and rip out images of children that call to you. Here are some aspects of our inner children that might like to be honored with a card: wounded, lonely, creative, magical, playful, happy, sad, rebellious, wounded, shy, frightened, guilty, shamed, secure. Are there other Inner Child voices that are important for you to honor with a card?

Journal with this question: *How can I be more faithful to my inner child this week?*

SoulCollage® Example

Please visit KaleidoSoul.com/into-the-heart-committee
The password for this page is: self

The topic to scroll down to is:
Inner Children

CHAPTER 9

My Singing Secret Self

A FEW MONTHS ago I was working with a group of friends on the "Secret Selves" exercise from Julia Cameron's book *Vein of Gold*. The idea was similar to SoulCollage® as it was helping us get in touch with some parts of us that we'd locked away, parts that were seeking full expression in our lives right then.

A few of my inner voices were willing to come forward at this point, and I was more than happy to listen. One part of me in particular seemed to be asking for attention. This is the part of me who loves performing as part of a group. I remembered in great detail just how much fun and excitement I always derived from singing in various choruses and glee clubs in high school and college.

This part of me told me that I'd shoved her aside when I graduated from college because I believed that fun things like that were over and done with once I became an "adult" in the "real" world. But lo and behold, this part of me was also telling me that wasn't the truth. She still passionately loves to sing. She still absolutely loves the idea of performing in a group, even though she is more than three decades out of college!

I've learned through this gentle practice of SoulCollage® to listen to, honor, and value *all* the parts of me, so I was able to give her a voice through journaling and meditation. I haven't found the right images to make a SoulCollage® card for her yet, but that isn't necessary for me to be aware of her, to listen to her, to try to meet her needs.

A few weeks after my Secret Singing Self made herself known to me, I received an email announcing that registration was open for the fall season of the Mystic Chorale, a large singing group in the Boston area whose mission is to *Make music a participatory experience, creating a dynamic collaboration among the bold and the shy, the untrained and the trained, the audience and the performers, challenging all of us to be truly amazing.*

I'm certain it was not a coincidence. I'm also certain that if I hadn't just done that "Secret Selves" exercise, I probably would have looked at the email invitation and brushed it off as something I might like to do but didn't really have time for. However, because I was so aware of this newly-remembered Singing Self, I paused and let myself read the whole email.

I was distinctly aware of this inner voice getting very excited about the possibility of singing with the Mystic Chorale. And yes, in case you're wondering . . . I signed up right then and there.

Time for Reflection

Devote some time to yourself this week. Ask some of your own "secret selves" to come forward. Are there some parts of you that were banished years ago? What parts of you are longing for fresh air and daylight again?

Create a SoulCollage® card for one of them. Let it speak.

Make some room in your life for it and watch what happens.

CHAPTER 10

Inquiring Minds Want to Know

A FRIEND WAS telling me a story the other day about something she'd heard on the news. A 600-pound moose had been seen wandering the streets of a small New Hampshire town. I kept interrupting her with questions. "Was it male or female?" "Was it from a zoo or was it wild?" "Don't moose travel in pairs or packs or families or something?" "Why was this moose all by itself?"

Finally, she looked at me and said, frustration seeping through her voice, "I just don't *know*! Stop asking me all these questions!"

I was so surprised, I had to pause. I hadn't even realized I was asking so many questions. Aha! I had just met the Curious Questioner, a part of me that I soon made a SoulCollage® card to honor (see link below).

In thinking back, I see that this *Curious Questioner* has always been a big part of my life. When someone is telling a story, I constantly interrupt them to ask questions. I seem to have this insatiable curiosity about everything I see and hear. I've noticed this about myself before, but I always connected it with the part of me who is a writer (details are important, you know!).

In noticing and honoring this part of me, I discovered that I really *like* her (in spite of her tendency to interrupt people while they're telling a story). Now I'm trying to use her energy to focus inward as well.

I recently heard Geneen Roth talk about using the process called Inquiry, which can be applied beautifully to our process with SoulCollage®. It's simple. Just start with a situation that is troubling or frustrating to you in some way, or look at a SoulCollage® card that reflects a part of yourself that is getting in your way. Then allow your Curious Questioner to start asking questions. It's important to remember that this curious part of you is completely impartial and nonjudgmental. It is driven only by a compassionate desire to know what's going on inside of you.

I find it works best to do this in my journal, as a dialog back and forth between the curious questioner and my inner wise self. I've been amazed at the answers that bubble forth simply because I asked the right questions!

Time for Reflection

Do you have a Curious Questioner inside of you? Set an intention to find some images for a SoulCollage® card for this part of you.

Listen inside during several minutes of intentional quiet this week. Is there something that this curious part of you is yearning to know? Make an effort to satisfy that longing.

Try an Inquiry dialog with a difficult situation or a part of you that's giving you trouble. Remember, the Curious Questioner only asks impartial, nonjudgmental questions during this dialog.

SoulCollage® Example

Please visit KaleidoSoul.com/into-the-heart-committee
The password for this page is: self

The topic to scroll down to is:
Inquiring Minds

CHAPTER 11

Guilt vs. Shame

I LEARNED A profound lesson about guilt and shame many years ago from an Episcopal priest. I had never thought much about the difference between these two feelings until he explained it in a sermon:

Guilt is saying "I *made* a mistake and I'm sorry."
Shame is saying "I *am* a mistake and I'm not worthy of forgiveness."

This lesson engraved itself on my heart, and I have taken it forward with me into my life. I now realize that it is *natural* and *necessary* to look at the mistakes I make and to feel guilty for making them. If I can admit my mistake and say I am sorry, then I can open to forgiveness, accept forgiveness, and move on.

I also realized that it's *not* natural and it's totally *unnecessary* for me to be ashamed of myself for a mistake I've made, or for a part of myself that I don't like, because shame makes me *less than myself*. Shame takes me away from myself. Shame makes opening to forgiveness impossible.

Time for Reflection

Take some time this week to meditate on and journal about the difference between guilt and shame as described above.

Make a SoulCollage® card that expresses how you feel when someone shames you, or when you feel ashamed of a mistake that you made.

Allow the person on the card to tell you his/her story.

The next time you make a serious mistake, acknowledge the guilt and say you are sorry to yourself or to whoever was affected by your mistake. Do not allow shame to weasel its way in by ignoring the guilt.

SoulCollage® Example

Please visit KaleidoSoul.com/into-the-heart-committee
The password for this page is: self

The topic to scroll down to is:
Shame

CHAPTER 12

Passion vs. Reason

IT SEEMS THAT at times there are two distinct voices inside of us. One is brave, daring, and passionate. *Yes! Yes! Let's fly a kite this morning, take a dance class, move to Wyoming, get a puppy.* The other is the one I call the Voice of Reason. *No! Wait! It looks like it might rain. You're too old and clumsy. You don't know anyone in Wyoming. You might be allergic to dogs.*

Sometimes these two voices can have quite an argument! Do you know what I mean? Have you heard them inside your head - the Passionate One and the Voice of Reason? Each of these Committee parts has something valid to say, and it's our job to listen. It's also our job to be a champion of the passionate part of ourselves, giving it room to spread its wings and fly.

Both parts are equally valid. It's up to us to keep clear boundaries and not let one overpower the other. The Voice of Reason wants to be heard; it needs to know that you are safe. The Passionate One needs air to breathe and space to take risks.

It's time to pay attention to what's going on inside of you. Who needs to be heard? Who needs room to breathe? And what can *you* do to ease this inner struggle?

Time for Reflection

If you could do anything, go anywhere, be anyone, what would that look like to you? What lights you up inside? What is your inner Passionate One urging you towards?

Is there an argument going on inside of you? Does the Voice of Reason seem to be winning over your Passionate One?

If you listen carefully to your Voice of Reason, can you discern why it is holding you back from following your passion? Is that part of you angry? Anxious? Frightened?

What steps can you take to lovingly reassure your Voice of Reason that you will keep it safe, no matter what?

Make a SoulCollage® card that honors the passionate part of you, and another one that represents the Voice of Reason. Ask each to state who it is and what it wants, then allow them to speak to each other. What are you learning from this inner dialog?

CHAPTER 13

Inner Dialogs

It is important to keep in mind when working with our Neters that they are not individual entities that exist in and of themselves. Each part of us is in relationship with the other parts.

This concept was made clear to me in a session with my therapist, Fran, when I was first beginning this inner work. She was guiding me through an imagery session where I was talking with my Inner Overachiever, who had been pretty much running my life with her to-do lists. I call this part of me Gabriella. She had been cracking the whip whenever I thought of taking a day (not to mention an hour) off.

Earlier in the session, I had been complaining to Fran about how my Inner Child, Julianna, never had time to do anything fun anymore. Now, after letting Gabriella talk for a while about all the things I had to do to get my business off the ground, Fran suggested that I ask her, "What do you think about Julianna?"

Without pausing a second, Gabriella replied, "Who? Are you saying that there is someone in here besides me?" She was actually horrified to realize that she wasn't the only one in my inner world!

This was a defining moment in my life because it brought home to me with resounding clarity the fact that my inner parts are indeed in relationship with each other, and that the stronger, more overbearing parts have the power to push the others out of the way, *if I am unaware of this imbalance.*

That's what it all comes down to: *awareness* and *balance.*

In this case, Gabriella *and* Julianna both needed a re-shifting of power. Gabriella needed a lot less; Julianna needed a lot more. It was my awareness of their relationship that was able to bring about that balance in my life.

Time for Reflection

To affect this balance, begin by dialoging with two of your cards, either intentionally (as I did, above) or randomly.

Choose a shadowed card (a Neter that is getting in your way right now) to work with. Then choose another card *intentionally* to dialogue with the first card. If you don't know how to get started, have the brighter card say *I Am the One Who . . .* and then let the shadowed Neter respond to that statement. Your dialogue will be off and running.

Choose a shadowed card (a Neter that is getting in your way right now) intentionally. Then choose another card *randomly* to dialog with it. Start the same way as described above, if you are having trouble getting started.

Choose two cards *randomly* from your deck and have them talk to each other about you, or about a third card.

Pose a question to your deck about something specific that is going on in your life right now. Draw seven cards and place them in a circle on the table in front of you. Write a conversation that these Neters are having *with each other* about the question you've posed about your life.

SoulCollage® Example

Please visit KaleidoSoul.com/into-the-heart-committee
The password for this page is: self

The topic to scroll down to is:
Inner Dialogs

CHAPTER 14

Wild Freedom

IN THE MOVIE *An Unfinished Life*, one of the central characters is a wild bear from the mountains of Wyoming. A rancher named Einar and his assistant have the misfortune of walking in on the bear while he is eating one of their livestock. The bear attacks the assistant, Mitch, leaving him terribly scarred, weak, and in constant pain. The local authorities hunt the bear and carry him off to the small local zoo where he is put in a metal cage that only serves to diminish his spirit.

Throughout the movie, Mitch continues to ask his boss to help the bear. "Go see if he's all right" becomes "feed him" which turns into "set him free." Einar thinks Mitch is crazy, but Mitch insists that the bear was only doing what bears do. He yearns desperately for the bear's freedom.

The bear is not the only character that is caged in this film, but he is the only one whose cage is visible. Einar is caged in his own mind, grieving the death of his only son as well as his wife's abandonment. His daughter-in-law (who lives with him) is caged inside her own lack of self-esteem. Mitch is caged inside his physical limitations due to the attack.

I won't tell you exactly what happens next in the film, but there is a scene near the end where the bear is loping through the mountains, lumbering as only a bear can. His cage is far behind him and his freedom seems like a clear strong bell that rings clearly in the wild, wide sky.

Time for Reflection

Is there a part of yourself that you have put in a cage, a part that you are afraid to set free?

Can you name this part of you? Try making a SoulCollage® card for it.

Do you have an inner Wild Woman or Wild Man who is trying to guide you to freedom? What does she/he look like? Try listening to what this voice is telling you.

What do the places of wild freedom inside of you look like? Give them image in a card.

SoulCollage® Example

Please visit KaleidoSoul.com/into-the-heart-committee
The password for this page is: self

The topic to scroll down to is:
Wild Freedom

CHAPTER 15

To Be or Not To Be . . . Patient

I HAVE STRUGGLED with patience all my life. When taking inventory of my "strong points" or "bright qualities," patience never makes it to the list! In fact, one of the very first SoulCollage® cards I made was for my impatient self (see link below). He is an impish yet angry little gremlin who says:

> *I Am the One Who can't wait, doesn't want to wait, and refuses to wait. I stomp my foot in anger because I'm in a hurry, dang it all! I can't wait to get to where I want to go. I will do anything to avoid long lines of traffic or waiting for anything, and it hurts my head to even think about it.*

Until I started practicing SoulCollage®, I didn't even think about what it might mean to cultivate patience, or to try and practice it once in a while. Then, after living with Mr. Impatience for a while, I decided to give image to the *tiny* piece of me who knows what it is to actually practice patience once in a while.

Here is what my Patient Self said to me when I first made the card to honor her: *I Am the One Who sits quietly and waits for whatever is coming on the horizon. I Am the One Who doesn't mind waiting. I Am the One Who is enjoying this moment, right now, and am not even thinking about what I am waiting for. Being in the moment is what makes it possible for me to be patient.*

That was a heart-opening moment for me, just listening to those words. I am now learning that the key to being more patient is not focusing on what I am waiting for, whether it's a test result from my doctor, a check in the mail, the release of the last ten pounds, or a vacation that

I'm looking forward to. The key to activating the energy of patience is being open to *this* present moment, right here, right now.

Another key to cultivating patience has to do with trust. In my own life, I activate patience much more easily if I can simply *trust* that the Universe is on my side, that all is well, that I will be given what I need (not necessarily what I want) no matter what. Life becomes easier then, and I am able to rest more fully in *this* moment instead of focusing on the future that I have been *impatiently* waiting for.

Time for Reflection

Do you have an impatient self? Find some images that bring that energy to mind and make a card for it. Do some journaling with it. Let it speak to you. What gifts does impatience have to give you? When does impatience serve you well? When does it get in your way?

What lessons have you learned about patience on your own journey? Is it easier to be patient at certain times? Make a card to honor the part of you that practices patience. Listen to what he/she has to teach you this week.

SoulCollage® Example

Please visit KaleidoSoul.com/into-the-heart-committee
The password for this page is: self

The topic to scroll down to is:
Patience

CHAPTER 16

You're As Sexy As You Think You Are

A COUPLE OF years ago, I explored my sexuality within the safe practice of SoulCollage® by making and working with two cards (see link below). At that time I was still recovering emotionally and physically from breast cancer surgeries and treatments. My body had been thrown into early menopause with the chemo treatments and "sexy" was just not a word that I related to anymore.

Right after making these cards, I read something in Denise Linn's book *Secrets and Mysteries: The Glory and Pleasure of Being a Woman* that really resonated with me. The author describes an acquaintance who isn't especially attractive (pocked skin, drooping shoulders) but who exuded a certain sexual radiance whenever she entered a room. Denise asked the woman if she knew why she had such a mesmerizing effect on people. Her response was, "I have a sense of my own style and my own presence. Even though I am insecure in many ways, I also know that I am a remarkable woman. Every woman has something about her that is amazing, but very few truly believe it. Even though I don't fit the normal view of beauty, I know I am desirable, radiant, and sensual. People are drawn to a woman who is comfortable with who she is."

That rang really true to my soul, and it is something that I am working towards in my own life. I believe that each of us really does have a Committee part who is as sexy as Marilyn Monroe, Jennifer Lopez, or whomever *you* consider sexy. My job is to coax this special part of me out of where she's been hiding in the shadows. She has been on the fringes of my being for way too long.

Time for Reflection

Take a look through your SoulCollage® cards. Do you have any cards that honor your own feelings about your sexuality, past or present? If not, seek out some images and create one or more.

If you're not ready for this yet, just set it all aside for a while and keep it in the back of your mind. When you're ready, the right images will make themselves known to you.

Do a reading with your deck. Ask, "Who has wisdom to give me about my sexuality today?" Draw three cards randomly. Listen to what they say. Remember that when we read from our decks, we do it only for ourselves. We never read our cards or anyone else's for someone else.

SoulCollage® Examples

Please visit kaleidosoul.com/sexuality

CHAPTER 17

The Truth Is . . .

I GREW UP with parents who instilled in me the importance of telling the truth. Because of this, I grew up with a positive moral conscience, and I'm thankful for that.

Looking back on my life now, however, I realize that I've been lying to myself. Even though I was very clear about telling the truth to others, I couldn't seem to tell it to myself. Here's a partial litany of the lies that some of my inner voices have been intent on telling me over the years:

You're not good enough.
You're unattractive.
People will leave you if you make a mistake.
You're a bad writer.
You can't live a joyful life because your mother was so wounded.
It's your fault you got breast cancer.
You should be afraid of failing.
Life is hard.

This began to change for me one weekend in 2004. My mother had died the previous month, and I was at a Kripalu retreat led by Tara Brach, whose book *Radical Acceptance* had begun to work its powerful way into my soul. She encouraged us to face and listen to some of these inner lies. When I heard them (really *heard* them), I felt inspired to begin to turn some of them around.

Kripalu has a beautiful outdoor labyrinth whose pathway is marked with over 90 small trees and low bushes. One sunny afternoon while I was there, I walked the labyrinth slowly, gently laying my hand on every bush and tree along the way. Every time I touched one, I said a *truth* about my life out loud. Not a lie, but a *truth*:

> *The truth is . . . my mother loved me even though she was wounded.*
> *The truth is . . . I can be whoever I want to be.*
> *The truth is . . . I love my husband.*
> *The truth is . . . my life is good.*
> *The truth is . . . lots of people love me.*
> *The truth is . . . I'm a good writer.*
> *The truth is . . . I've learned lots of things about myself because I had breast cancer.*
> *The truth is . . . I'm a good person.*

What a Blessing Walk! That ritual was so powerful, so astounding, that it still remains with me to this day. I felt such sweet, grounded joy saying those truths out loud. All I have to do now is close my eyes and remember the feel of the soft ground beneath my feet, the prickly touch of the bushes against my palm, the scent of grassy mountain air . . . and I can feel the power of these truths beating within my chest, at home in my soul, right where they belong.

Time for Reflection

Listen inside to your own inner voices. Are any of them hell-bent on telling you lies also? Take some time to write some of these lies in your journal.

Read them out loud.

Find some time to do your own version of "The Truth Is . . ." ritual. Allow the power of these new truths to sink into your body, mind, and spirit.

Draw a few SoulCollage® cards and ask each one to tell you what the truth is. You might be pleasantly surprised!

CHAPTER 18

Reading, Uninterrupted

AT ONE POINT in my life, I had a part time job at a large bookstore near my home, and my inner book lover jumped up and down for joy. Books, books, and more books were the order of the days that I worked there. I saw, smelled, and touched books for hours on end, days at a time. Sometimes it seemed like I was in heaven!

Also, to my inner Book Lover's delight, the break room at that bookstore was always full of people. Were they chatting and gossiping like those on break in other jobs I'd had? No siree! They were all *reading*! I felt right at home because I was surrounded by fellow book lovers.

I made my Book Lover card early on my SoulCollage® journey (see link below). She has shown up several times in my daily readings to remind me that reading books is one of the things that always grounds me and brings me home to myself.

My parents read to me from the time I was a baby, and I learned early on the value of books as a gateway to the imagination. When I was in first grade, my mother started reading *The Wizard of Oz* to me, one chapter at a time. I was anxiously awaiting the final chapter but when she wasn't able to read it to me the first time I asked, I finished the book myself. Mom loved to tell that story about me when I got older!

When I go on vacation, you'll find at least six books in my suitcase (sometimes more) because this is my idea of the ideal vacation: hours and hours of reading, uninterrupted.

When my stepchildren's kids were born, we gave them (and continue to give them) books, rather than blankets or toys. Let the other grandparents give them those trinkets. My husband and I are giving them a gift far deeper and grander: we are giving them the love of reading.

Time for Reflection

Is there a Book Lover on your own inner Committee? If so, be sure to create a card for him/her in your deck.

If you already have a Book Lover card, take it out of your deck and let it speak to you this week.

Are you reading enough lately? Too much? Not enough?

Ask this Neter how you can spread the love of reading to someone else during the coming months.

SoulCollage® Example

Please visit KaleidoSoul.com/into-the-heart-committee
The password for this page is: self

The topic to scroll down to is:
Book Lover

CHAPTER 19

Don't Mess with Me

A FEW YEARS ago I read an interview with Glenn Close and was astonished to discover that she still has the infamous carving knife from the film *Fatal Attraction*. Not only does she have it, but it is hanging on the wall in her kitchen! She told the journalist that it was her way of reminding herself not to let anyone mess with her.

The knife from the film *Fatal Attraction*. This invokes a strong image in my mind. Can you picture it in your imagination? Heavy silver metal. Dark wooden handle. Forever stained with blood.

What if we each had something like that hanging in our own kitchens? A visceral, shocking symbol that would remind us that we do indeed have a part inside of us who says, "Don't mess with me." It doesn't have to be as gruesome as a bloody knife. Maybe you could use a picture of a mother bear protecting her cubs, or a shield with a warrior painted on it. Perhaps your personal "Fatal Attraction Knife" could be a small bow and arrow set, a toy ax, or a picture of a mother with her arms tightly around her child.

Whatever it is, remember its message is *protection*, not destruction. Find a way to honor that fierce warrior who lives inside of you and whose only task is to say, "Don't mess with me" to anyone who tries to hurt you in any way.

Time for Reflection

How does your Inner Warrior protect you? Do you have a SoulCollage® card for this powerful part of you? Make a commitment to look for images that represent him or her.

Create a new card to honor this "Don't Mess with Me" voice. Then let it speak to you.

Revel in its presence. Allow it to protect you.

SoulCollage® Example

Please visit KaleidoSoul.com/into-the-heart-committee
The password for this page is: self

The topic to scroll down to is:
Don't Mess with Me

CHAPTER 20

You're Bigger Than They Are

WHEN MY BELOVED cat Sasha was only a kitten, it was always a struggle to clip her claws. Armed with a pair of nail clippers, I proceeded cautiously, fearful of injuring her. What always ensued was a tussle, a struggle, a veritable melee: me versus the kitten . . . with the kitten emerging as champion. Sasha managed to squirm away, and her claws thus kept growing longer and sharper. Ouch.

Several months into these failed, fearful attempts at claw-snipping, we went to the vet for Sasha's yearly check-up. Dr. Friedman commented on how long her claws were, so I proceeded to tell him how hard it was to cut them. "She's always squirming around," I explained. "I'm afraid of hurting her. She just won't sit still, and then she runs away from me."

Even though this was many years ago, I remember our vet's kind response to this day. He stopped me in midsentence, put his hand up, palm facing me like a stop sign, then said, "I think you're forgetting something. *You're bigger than she is.*"

His words stopped my self-defeating thoughts right in their well-grooved tracks. Could it possibly be that simple? I *am* bigger than she is. I *can* hold her still! After that day I was able to do it easily and effortlessly. Claw-trimming time became a time of cuddling, and my Sasha-girl sat still for it every week for the rest of her long, loving life.

As I think about this story now, I see that maybe it can be like this in my inner world as well. Oftentimes, I hear myself whining and complaining that certain inner voices (Queen Puritanica, the Overeaters, Ethel, my Inner Critic . . . etc.) have taken over again. When this happens, I feel helpless and out of control.

But when I think about this now in light of what I learned from our vet, I realize something important. Yes, I am certainly bigger than my little animal friends, but isn't it true that "I" am also bigger than each of my inner parts? Isn't it absolutely true that "I" am the one who is in charge? Me. ME! I am the one who decides what goes on inside of me in the long run, don't I? So why do I let these shadowed inner voices sometimes get the better of me? Is it fear or just old habits?

Maybe it's simply that I've forgotten a very simple truth: *I am bigger than they are.*

If "I" am not strong enough yet to talk back to these parts of myself, then maybe I can ask a different, brighter, stronger part of myself to converse with them instead. There are many wise, clear parts of my inner world who *can* do this: the Wise One, the Smart One, the Good Mother, and the Priestess, to name a few. Try it yourself and see.

Time for Reflection

Choose an area of your life where a shadowed inner voice has "taken over." This voice could represent anger, fear, or something more specific like overeating or overspending.

Allow this part to "speak" to you, telling you exactly what it thinks and feels, what it wants and doesn't want. Don't hold it back. Truly, let it have its say. It's okay if you don't have a SoulCollage® card for this part of yourself yet, but you might consider creating one eventually.

Now flip through your deck until you find a brighter, stronger part of yourself.

Write a conversation between these two parts. Allow the part that has been in control to tell you its own story. Then invite the bright part to say what needs to be said to the darker part.

CHAPTER 21

My Bodacious Bod

I CREATED A SoulCollage® card (see link below) to honor the part of me who loves my body no matter what I look like. This is the part of me who walks with confidence no matter how much I weigh. I was originally drawn to the three central images, and then the card flew together and practically created itself.

Now let me make it clear that I don't *always* walk like this, and I don't *always* love my body unconditionally. I struggled for years with emotional eating and a poor body image. However, I keep this card in my deck to remind me that this part of me does indeed exist, even though it has been given little attention for so long.

I encourage you as the days go by to listen to your own inner voices. Is there a part of you who is proud of *your* precious body, no matter what it looks like, no matter what scars it bears or how many wrinkles it is blessed with?

Honor that part with a card.

Time for Reflection

Make a list of ways that you can honor your body this week. Choose one of them and do it today.

Stand in front of a full-length mirror and admire yourself. Look into your own eyes. Say kind and loving things to yourself, out loud.

Allow a SoulCollage® card to bloom from some piece of this inner work.

SoulCollage® Example

Please visit KaleidoSoul.com/into-the-heart-committee
The password for this page is: self

The topic to scroll down to is:
Bodacious Bod

CHAPTER 22

Changing the Rules

I HAD A long talk the other day with my inner Rule Maker whom I call Queen Puritanica. I first heard of this voice while reading *Embracing Your Inner Critic* by Hal and Sidra Stone. They referenced the inner Rule Maker in connection with what they call the Tricky Triangle, which is made up of three inner Committee parts: the rule maker, the perfectionist, and the inner critic.

The idea is that if my Inner Critic (whom I lovingly call Ethel) is acting out and really nagging me with negative criticism, she isn't working alone! The whole process of criticizing me starts with the Rule Maker, the one who made the rules. The Perfectionist is all about obsessively following the rules that the Rule Maker created. I call mine Perfectionista. And the Inner Critic? Well, when the Perfectionist falls short (and she usually does), the Inner Critic starts right in with her angry critiques.

I was experiencing a whole lot of this inner verbal abuse from Ethel a few weeks ago. And I was listening. But, after years of doing this deep inner work, I found that I was actually aware of her separate voice, and this time I wasn't buying into it. I remembered the Tricky Triangle and decided to go back to the source of this inner misery: the Rule Maker.

I had a little chat with this Neter in my journal. I let her talk for a while and this is some of what she said: *I Am the One Who makes the rules. I don't make them up out of thin air, you know. I make them for your own benefit. I Am the One Who makes the rules to keep you in line, to keep you from being hurt or ridiculed or embarrassed. I Am the One Who decides what the rules are. This is who I am. And I use Perfectionista and Ethel to help you follow the rules.*

At that point I thanked her for keeping order in my inner world and then asked her, "What exactly are the rules you've made for me that I've been following all these years?"

Here is what she told me:

1. Thou shalt be thin.
2. Thou shalt have a flat stomach.
3. Thou shalt not take pleasure in food lest you gain back the weight you've already lost.
4. Thou shalt not rock the boat.
5. Thou shalt compare yourself to everyone else to see where you are lacking.
6. Thou shalt take action based on what others think or might think about you.
7. Thou shalt struggle because life is hard.
8. Thou shalt act on the assumption that something bad is always just around the corner.

Looking at this list, I could plainly see how she'd been operating behind the radar throughout my life. In fact, many of these rules came from my childhood, from my own parents' belief system. It was truly enlightening to make this list with my inner Rule Maker, Queen Puritanica!

After several more minutes of journaling with her about these rules, I came to the conclusion that if I am truly the author of this story that is my life, then I have the right to *change the script*. I suddenly realized that I am the one who can change the rules! So I came up with a new list, one each to change the shape of a previous one, and then a new one just for me:

1. Thou shalt appreciate thy body whatever its shape and size.
2. Thou shalt love all parts of thy body unconditionally.

3. Thou shalt take pleasure in food without overindulging.
4. Thou shalt steer the boat to the best of your ability, knowing that sometimes boats must rock in order to get to where they are going.
5. Thou shalt compare thyself only to thyself.
6. Thou shalt listen within and act on that inner direction.
7. Thou shalt relax because when life is hard, you will have Assistance.
8. Thou shalt surrender to the flow of your life.
9. Thou shalt celebrate and take pleasure in all of your gifts.

I don't know if that is the end of the new rule-making. There may be more waiting to be written. For now, I am satisfied with these. The tricky triangle inside of me is much more peaceful now. Perfectionista finds these rules easy to follow, and Ethel has much less to criticize because of this.

Time for Reflection

Have you listened inside for your own tricky triangle? What do these voices say to you?

Listen carefully for a few days to your own inner Rule Maker. Make a list of several rules that it has been dictating to you for years. Notice which of these rules are out of date.

Journal a conversation with your inner Rule Maker about where these rules came from.

Bring your inner Wise Ones to a Committee meeting in your imagination and come up with a new set of rules for yourself.

Post these rules where you'll see them often. Memorize them! Work with them daily until they are as much a part of you as the old rules were.

SoulCollage® Example

Please visit KaleidoSoul.com/into-the-heart-committee
The password for this page is: self

The topic to scroll down to is:
Tricky Triangle

Shadow

Overview

In the practice of SoulCollage®, we define a shadowed Neter as one that is out of balance in some way. There might be too much of a particular Neter's energy, or too little of it. This shadow often shows up within the Committee as parts of ourselves that hold us back, make us unhappy, or get in our way. These are inner parts that usually make us feel ashamed or embarrassed; they are parts that we tend to hide from ourselves and others. Examples might be: Compulsive Spender, Overeater, Angry One, Anxiety, Depression, Impatience, Lonely Laura. These will vary from person to person, so take a look inside and notice which shadowed parts belong to you. This is the first step towards balance and wholeness.

The SoulCollage® process encourages us to work with our personal shadowed Neters in a threefold process. First we become aware of our shadowed parts (parts that are not wholly conscious); we name them and honor them with cards. Next we begin to know them, and bring them into balance. We do this by dialoguing with each one, and listening compassionately to its story without judgment or criticism. During this part of the process we may actually discover this part's gift, or positive intent. Finally, we accept these shadowed Neters and make space for them in our lives. The amazing thing is that the shadowed parts become less excessive and less troublesome once we bring them into the light.

CHAPTER 23

Naming Our Personal Shadowed Parts

LEARNING ABOUT OUR personal shadowed parts is a powerful tool for self-discovery, particularly when viewed through the light of SoulCollage®. Here are some definitions of personal shadow that might resonate with you:

- Our shadow contains all the parts of us that we are not at peace with. (Debbie Ford)
- Our shadow consists of parts that we have sent into the basement of our subconscious. (Carl Jung)
- Shadowed parts are parts of myself that:

  - hold me back
  - make me unhappy
  - get in my way
  - make me feel embarrassed or ashamed
  - tend to be hidden

Some of my own shadowed parts include: Negative Nancy, Angry Annie, Misunderstood Martha, Queen of Denial, Chameleon, Hiding Away, and my Inner Critic Ethel. Trust me, there are plenty more!

The SoulCollage® approach to working with these shadowed parts is to name them, befriend them, and claim them. We are to meet them and bless them with kindness and compassion. We are to accept them exactly as they are. Seena talks about *carrying* them rather than *curing* them. We are to be grateful for them, although this may be easier with some than with others. The basic premise is that these inner shadowed parts become less excessive and less troublesome once they are brought into the light of our consciousness.

A huge shift took place in my life when I realized that I wasn't supposed to *change or fix* any of these shadowed parts, but to simply *accept* them as they are and then begin to bring them into balance.

Time for Reflection

The first step in working with our personal shadowed parts is to simply *name* some of them. That's it!

Use the Shadowy Parts Worksheet (see link below) to start naming some of your own shadowed parts. Remember, this is *not* about beating yourself up. You don't need to go out right this minute and make a SoulCollage® card for every shadowy part that is inside of you! This is just an exercise in self-observation.

Also, please remember that our mission here is not to seize up with panic when looking at our lists. It might be tempting to think that you need to change or fix these parts of yourself, but that is not our goal. Do this work with the intention of simply *naming* and *accepting* these parts of you.

SoulCollage® Resource

The Shadowy Parts Worksheet is here:
kaleidosoul.com/shadow-handouts

CHAPTER 24

Befriending Our Shadowed Parts

IN ORDER TO get to the gift or the "positive intent" that one of these shadowed parts offers, we need to spend some actual *time* with it. We're not going to find the gift or the light in that shadowed part if we keep it at arm's length, or if we push it away. This part of the process is called "befriending."

To do this, you need to choose a shadowed part that you want to work with. Then you're going to take some steps towards it with befriending in mind. We always do this part *slowly* and *gently*.

Last year I read a wonderful novel, *The Lion Is In* by Delia Ephron. In the story, three women come upon a billiard hall in the desert. There's a lion in a cage inside. He's an old lion who has been kicked out of the circus, and the manager thinks the lion will draw a crowd to his business. However, he is so afraid of the lion that he doesn't know what to do with it.

One of the three women is very drawn to the energy of this lion, even though it seems sad and is just moping around. She eventually befriends it. The process goes very slowly. She doesn't just charge up to him and expect to become friends all at once. She goes through the process of very slowly making the lion feel safe with her. She begins by simply pulling up a chair and sitting in silence in the room with him, first for five minutes, then for longer amounts of time.

When I read this novel, it reminded me of a stray cat who appeared on our front porch during the summer of 2011. We had never seen him around before and he would run away if we came close to him. We named him Raj because he looked so majestic. I noticed that once we stopped trying to run after him, he kept coming back. He let us feed him and he liked sleeping on one of our comfy porch chairs.

I wanted to pet him to show him that I loved him, so I got him to be comfortable with me by just standing a few feet away from him and talking to him softly. I had to do this for a couple of weeks. After that I moved a little closer while talking to him. He just looked at me with his big green eyes. After a month or two of that, he let me pet him on the head for just one second, and then the next time a little bit longer. Eventually he even let me stroke his back lightly once in a while.

My point is that in order to befriend one of your personal shadowed parts, you need to do it *gently* and *slowly*. If it's a part of you that's been out of balance for a really long time, you will need to get it to feel safe with you again.

Thich Nhat Hanh suggests a beautiful phrase that we can say to ourselves whenever we're feeling sad, angry or out of balance in any way: *Dear One, I am here for you.* This is the kind of energy we want to project towards our own inner shadowed parts when they get in our way, or when we notice them taking up too much space in our minds and hearts. *Dear one, I am here for you.*

Time for Reflection

One of the ways you can start to befriend a shadowed part is by finding images and making a card to honor it.

Next, journal and dialog with this shadowed part. Allow this Neter to tell you about itself in its own words. Here are some suggestions for questions you can ask: Who are you? How did you get to be here? Who put you here? What is your real job in my life?

A big part of the befriending process is going slowly and not expecting that you're going to develop an immediate rapport (although you might).

SoulCollage® Examples

An important part of my own journey with shadow is how I was able to help my inner shaming part (Malfoy) transform into a wise teacher (Lucius). Take a few minutes to read the story of that transformation and see if it makes the taming of one of your own shadowed parts any easier:

kaleidosoul.com/story
The password for this page is: malfoy

CHAPTER 25

Embracing Your Inner Villains

I SAW *SHREK the Third* recently and found much in it that relates to our personal shadows. Besides being flat out funny, this movie also has a very imaginative subplot to which all avid SoulCollagers should pay attention.

In this subplot, Prince Charming is upset because he hasn't gotten his own "happily ever after." He makes his way to the Poison Apple Bar (don't you love it?!?) and finds a diverse group of storybook "villains" who have been banished forever from the Kingdom. Now just try to imagine this: every "bad" character you've ever come across in a story has been sent to a dark, dreary land, and they are not happy about it! These "villains" include: a Big Bad Wolf, a Wicked Stepmother, Captain Hook, an Evil Queen, the Cyclops, Rumpelstiltskin, Mabel the Ugly Stepsister, the Headless Horseman, assorted Black Knights, and Magical Evil Trees (remember The Wizard of Oz?).

The villains are angry and unhappy because they feel that *no one has ever listened to their side of the story.*

Read that sentence over again because it is extremely important! The villainous characters have been banished from the Kingdom, and they are furious and miserable because *they have not been allowed to tell their side of the story.*

Immediately, this storyline makes me think of my own inner Queendom and of all the shadowy, villainous parts of my Self that I tend to banish from my general field of vision. I really love the happy-bright and shiny-perky little parts of my Self, (who doesn't?) and am always more than ready to listen to them. But I don't like looking at the dreadful and unpleasant pieces of my psyche. I don't often sit down with my own inner Captain Hook, my secret Evil Queen, my buried Black Knight, my concealed Ugly Stepsister . . . or any of them.

Why? Because they scare the heck out of me!

Frankly, who wants to admit that they have an "Evil Queen" in their inner family, an inner part who sometimes is full of hate and longs to get her hands on a poisoned apple? Who wants to acknowledge that there's a Big Bad Wolf who takes over their personality and bites peoples' heads off now and then? If there's a felon or "crazy" person in your family tree, you're probably not going to talk about them with everyone who crosses your path. Best to keep family members like that hidden from view. And guess what? We do the exact same thing with our inner family, our inner Committee.

I have found that the only way to make peace with these villainous parts is to:

1. Become aware of them.
2. Visualize and name them,
3. Sit down and listen to their side of the story.

This three-step process is much easier said than done, of course, but we have such a marvelous gift in SoulCollage®. Through the creative process and our SoulCollage® cards, we can become more aware of these shadowed parts of ourselves. We give each part an image or maybe a name, and then through the *I Am The One Who . . .* exercise, we sit down and let that part of us speak. One of the biggest gifts of SoulCollage® is that it allows our villainous, hidden-away parts to open up and tell their stories in safety.

This kind of inner work takes time, gentleness and an inner acceptance that isn't always easy for me, so I have learned to allow it time and space. But I have found that when I pay attention to an inner villain, when I can put aside my fear, sit down and really listen, then that inner villain becomes less like a villain and more like a friend.

Meanwhile, back at *Shrek the Third*, Prince Charming (who also has been banished for being too perfect) convinces all the storybook villains to join him in battle for their own "happy ever after." This isn't just a children's movie. Watch it and see for yourself!

Time for Reflection

Look again at the list of storybook villains listed above. Do any of them resonate with your own inner world? Are there any more that need to be added to your list? Make a list of some of your own shadowed qualities that make you uncomfortable (some of mine include: selfishness, a quick temper, and negativity).

Seek out images to use on a SoulCollage® card for one of them. Remember, these shadowed parts are not to be feared!

SoulCollage® Resource

Visit this page for more information about the *I Am the One Who . . .* exercise:

kaleidosoul.com/soulcollage-cards-interpreting

CHAPTER 26

Another Way of Seeing

Perhaps all the dragons in our lives
are only princesses waiting for us to act,
just once, with beauty and courage.
Perhaps everything that frightens us is,
in its deepest essence,
something helpless that wants our love.

~RILKE

A FEW YEARS ago some friends and I went to see the Broadway musical *Wicked*. Based in part on the novel by Gregory Maguire, *Wicked* tells the real story of the Wicked Witch in the beloved children's story *The Wizard of Oz*.

In the beginning, the Wicked Witch (Elphaba) wasn't wicked. She happened to be born green, a source of shame to her otherwise "normal" family. She had no friends until she went away to college. There she met Glinda, who turned out to be the "good" witch.

Elphaba was actually kind, intelligent, and compassionate. There was quite a lot that happened to make her appear so "wicked." In fact, even in her most "wicked" moments, the audience knows that she isn't wicked at all. It's simply a matter of the stories that are being told about her; it's a matter of how she's being perceived that gives her the label "wicked."

At one point, she and a fellow classmate (Fiero) are falling in love. He tells her she is beautiful.

"No, I'm not beautiful. You're lying," she replies, looking away from him.

"It's not lying," Fiero replies passionately. "It's another way of seeing."

And *that*, my friend, is the essence of the story: another way of seeing. Fiero had taken the time to really *see* Elphaba, and in looking beneath her green skin, he touched the truer beauty that lay beneath.

This applies to our own inner lives as well. There is another way of seeing the "wicked" parts of our own personalities, another way of seeing what we have until now perceived as dragons. As Rilke says in the quotation above, with courage and love we can now see those "dragons" as hurt beings in need of our tender loving care. It just takes a bit of time, a lot of curiosity and . . . *another way of seeing.*

If *you* have an inner Wicked Witch, don't try to melt her with your shame and self-judgment. Invite her to tell you *her* story. Listen as she tells you *how* she got to be so "wicked." Try, if just for a moment, to see her in another way, a kinder way. You just might discover that she's not as wicked as you thought. You just might find her beautiful too.

Time for Reflection

Create a SoulCollage® card for your own inner Wicked Witch, or whatever you call her (or him). Mine is Ethel, my Inner Critic. Journal with this Neter using the four basic questions (see link below).

After your initial journaling, ask this Neter some other questions: What are you most afraid of? How are you trying to help me? When did you first appear in my life?

If you already have a card for this part of you, spend some time this week dialoging with it. Pay attention to when and where in your life this voice blocks you from being your brightest self.

SoulCollage® Resource

Visit this page for more information about the journaling activity mentioned above:

kaleidosoul.com/soulcollage-cards-interpreting

CHAPTER 27

Who's Locked Up in Your Inner Dungeon?

SOMETIMES I VISUALIZE all my inner Committee parts residing in a big castle. Each one has its own room, and sometimes I imagine myself there, exploring the various rooms and meeting up with the part of me that inhabits each one.

One day a few weeks ago while "exploring" my inner castle, I found myself in the cold, gloomy dungeon. I discovered that there are parts of me I've hidden down there because other parts have been stronger, or because I just haven't known how to interact with them.

Angry Annie is one of those parts. I am getting to know her a little bit better day by day.

She has given me some very interesting information as I've been working with her. For example, she reminded me that I didn't exactly grow up with very good role models for expressing anger. My mother lashed out with hers; my father kept his under lock and key. Angry Annie helped me to see that I chose to follow my father's anger pattern because it wasn't as hurtful to others.

The most exciting revelation, however, came when I asked Angry Annie, "What do you have to give me?" She replied: *I give you a signal that something isn't right in your world. I give you the knowledge that anger is okay and acceptable. I give you a sense of responsibility to try to fix whatever is making you angry. I give you energy to right wrongs and to speak up for yourself in situations where no one is listening to you.*

One day last week I imagined myself taking her hand in the dungeon and inviting her to go with me "upstairs" into my world and into my life. What a difference it made!

It just so happened that that very same day, my husband did something that deeply angered me. This was not just surface stuff being activated, but many years of stepfamily issues rising to the surface. As I felt my blood begin to boil, I remembered that Angry Annie was beside me for the day. It was as if she really had been set free. I was able to speak my anger to my husband without being consumed by it, a new and healthy experience for me.

Time for Reflection

Make a commitment to pay attention to your own inner Angry One this week. Are you comfortable allowing this Neter to walk through your day with you, or is it locked up in your own inner dungeon? Give this part of you a name, if you like, and begin a conversation.

Find a way to honor this angry voice inside of you. You might make a SoulCollage® card for it, spend a few minutes listening to it in a journaled dialog, or simply make a little extra room for it in the "upstairs" of your soul.

If this whole idea of an inner castle and dungeon intrigues you, I challenge you to take your inner Wise Self with you and go down to that dungeon. Notice, just notice if there are any other parts of you locked up down there.

SoulCollage® Example

Please visit KaleidoSoul.com/into-the-heart-shadow
The password for this page is: shadow

The topic to scroll down to is:
Dungeon

CHAPTER 28

Welcoming and Entertaining the Shadows

FULLY-GROWN MEN HAD become mean bullies: taunting and beating up a nice young man while demolishing his brand new car. I got the shivers every time I saw them. Okay, it was only a production of *Ragtime* at the theatre where I used to work. But I still got the shivers. They were so mean. I knew they were only actors portraying characters according to the script's direction, but whenever *those* characters came onstage, I wanted to run and hide!

Having seen *Ragtime* several times, I was totally amazed at these actors' ability to portray such cruelty over and over again. One day I found occasion to ask them if it was difficult doing that scene night after night, if it took a lot of energy to summon up that intense level of malicious brutality so often.

"Nah," one of them said off-handedly, and the rest of them nodded agreement as he explained. "It's easy getting *into* the role. What's really hard is getting *out* of it when the show's over."

I was astounded. These actors were all really nice young men. I had thought they were going to tell me how difficult it was to get into the mindset of these vicious, racist, mean-hearted characters. But they were telling me it wasn't hard at all. They were telling me they actually even enjoyed it a bit, to the point of forgetting who they really were.

This all took place many years before I had ever heard of SoulCollage®. But my question and their response has stayed with me all this time, and I have brought it up in my mind many times since then, turning it around and around, looking at it from different angles, trying to make sense of it.

71

Now that I'm practicing SoulCollage®, I more fully understand what those actors were trying to say. *No one* is exempt from meanness and cruelty. We *all* have the capacity for questionable behavior. We *all* have parts of ourselves that we don't like. And we, like those actors, can shift into these shadowy mindsets at a moment's notice (sometimes even *without* notice).

The most important thing is being *aware* of these different parts of ourselves and not forgetting who we really are at our deepest core.

Time for Reflection

Make a short list of some parts of yourself that you don't like. These are usually parts that get in the way of allowing yourself to remember and act from who you really are. It's important not to spend too much time on your list as it might make you feel overwhelmed. Try listing just a few for now.

Next, start searching for images that represent these parts of your inner world. It might take a while, or you might already have some images saved up.

Make a card to honor one of these inner parts.

Ask this part: *Who are you? What do you have to give me? What do you want from me? Are you related to any other members of my inner family? When did you come into being?* Listen to the answers. Accept whatever this voice has to tell you. The object is not to make this part of you disappear. The object is to give this part of you what it most needs and wants from you - validation and acceptance.

CHAPTER 29

Gifts From The Parts We Don't Like

WHEN I FIRST started SoulCollage®, the hardest thing for me to understand was the fact that my hidden, scary parts had something good to give me. I struggled with this for a long time until I discovered a part of me that I'd long since locked in "the basement" of my soul.

Meet Maggie. She's the sad woman on a card I made for the part of me who cries easily, who grieves easily, and who feels deep sorrow (see link below). I discovered this part of me when stumbling across the image of the sad woman on the couch, hugging a pillow to her chest. I named her "Maggie" because I was watching a television series at the time, and a large storyline revolved around a sorrowful character with that name.

My therapist did some guided visualizations where she led me through inner conversations with Maggie. During one of these sessions, I had a very big "aha" moment. There is a reason why I grieve so deeply; there is a reason why I cry so easily. It is because I have such a big, loving heart.

This was a major revelation! I had always been ashamed of the fact that I cry so quickly, and feel things so intensely, but I'd never thought to seek the *gift* in this part of myself.

When I realized this, I went in search of an image to represent "Maggie's" big heart. Now my card represents so much more to me than just sadness and grief; it shows me the light within the darkness.

I find that I am much more comfortable now with the part of me who cries easily and feels so deeply. Just last night I had a sudden thought about Scooter, the affectionate tiger cat we lost in 2006. I think about him often, but last night my memories were accompanied by a vast well-spring of sorrow. It took me unawares. Before I knew it, tears were streaming down my face.

At first, I heard Ethel, my Inner Critic, saying, "It's been a long time, for heaven's sake! You don't need to be crying about that silly cat anymore."

But then I caught myself. "No," I said to Ethel. "Maggie needs to cry. We loved Scooter, and we're just not done crying yet." So I cried. Eventually I felt better. Eventually I stopped crying.

Maggie is an integral part of me now. I have accepted this part of me that I used to be ashamed of. I have listened to her and embraced her. I have given her space in my soul.

Time for Reflection

Intentionally dialog with one of your inner parts who makes you uncomfortable. Do this in your imagination and/or in your journal. Continue the dialog until you find the gift that this part brings to you.

The gifts *are* there. May we all search for them. May we find them, embrace them, and bless them.

SoulCollage® Example

Please visit KaleidoSoul.com/into-the-heart-shadow
The password for this page is: shadow

The topic to scroll down to is:
Maggie

CHAPTER 30

Quieting Those Inner Naysayers

THE DICTIONARY DEFINES *naysayer* as "someone with an aggressively negative attitude." It comes from the ancient word *nay*, which means *no*. I don't know about you, but I have quite a few of these Naysayers in my inner world, and I've given image to them in my deck. One is Negative Nancy. Others include Queen Puritanica and Ethel, my Inner Critic. There are several more, of course, and it feels to me that they are all related. Indeed, they form an inner family of sorts, and sometimes they all gang up on me, which can leave me feeling unhappy and isolated.

Over the years of working with my Inner Naysayers, I have found that the best way of *quieting* them is by *listening* to them. You may be wondering how they will ever quiet down unless they are forcibly silenced, but there's a beautiful paradox that we discover within SoulCollage® when working with shadowed parts like this. When the Naysayers are given room to speak, when we really listen to them, they calm down, and they stop hitting us over the head with their painfully sharp hammers. We have to give them time to tell us their stories!

A few years ago, a conference center called to say they were cancelling a workshop I'd scheduled because no one had signed up. I was immediately aware of these Inner Naysayers ganging up on me. They were saying things like this: *See, I told you so. No one wants to come to your workshops. You'll never be successful at this business. Give it up.*

At first it was tempting to give in to the Naysayers, to think badly of myself, to not schedule any more workshops. But I chose to slow down and listen to them; I decided to give them some space. As I listened, I discovered that they were deeply afraid of failing, and because of this, they were trying to protect me from the pain of not succeeding. Once I realized this,

I was able to understand their pronounced negativity. "I know you're upset because they cancelled the workshop," I said to the Naysayers (in my imagination). "But that's just one workshop. It doesn't mean we're going to fail. Let's look instead at the two other workshops that people *are* signing up for. Let's look at the successful workshop we led last month."

Once these negative energies in my mind realized I had heard and understood them, they quieted right down and I was able to go ahead with the planning of future workshops.

Time for Reflection

Is there a family of Naysayers in your inner world? Do you have SoulCollage® cards for them? If so, pull them out of your deck, spread them before you, and notice how they are related. Journal about times in your life when you gave them power to stop you from doing something you really wanted to do.

Is there a situation in your life right now that is bringing out these Naysayers? Go to your journal and allow at least one of them some room to tell you its story. Ask it why it is streaming negativity towards you today. Remember, you can do this even if you don't have a SoulCollage® card for this Neter yet.

If you don't have any SoulCollage® cards for your inner Naysayers, start looking for images that might reflect their energy in your life. Put together a card when you feel like you are ready.

SoulCollage® Example

Please visit KaleidoSoul.com/into-the-heart-shadow
The password for this page is: shadow

The topic to scroll down to is:
Naysayers

CHAPTER 31

The Upside of Anger

I GREW UP in an ordinary family where I was wanted and loved by both my parents and my two older brothers. However, even in a loving family of origin such as this, I learned a few unhealthy things growing up. One such lesson was about anger.

Neither of my parents expressed anger in healthy ways. My mother lashed out at people with hers; she hurt people with it. As for my dad, I never once saw him express anger. He was the calm to my mother's storm. He was soft-spoken and gentle. The subconscious lesson I learned way back then was that my father's way of dealing with anger was better. After all, he may have stuffed it down and suppressed it, but he didn't hurt people with it either.

As the years went by, there were things that happened that made me angry, but mostly I just stuffed my anger down like my father had. Along the way I had read some things about "healthy ways to deal with anger," but I was a little baffled about this because I hadn't had any good role models.

In 1991 I met my husband, Jeff, and moved in with him and his two older children, Amanda (10) and Jeffrey (7). As you may have guessed, there were a lot more opportunities for me to learn about expressing anger when living in the midst of a stepfamily! It was becoming clearer and clearer to me that anger was an energy inside of me. The first thing I learned is that it was perfectly okay to *feel* it! I also learned that I could allow the energy of anger to hurt myself and others, or I could use it for good. I slowly figured out ways to express my anger to Jeff and the kids in simple ways that allowed them to know I still loved them.

The biggest lesson I learned about anger was when Amanda was in 7th grade. She had strep throat and was told by her doctor to stay home from school for a week. When I went into her school on the second day and asked for her homework assignments, I was told they couldn't give them to me because I wasn't part of her family. I argued with them for a while, but they were adamant. It was "school policy." There were "rules" about these things.

Well, the word anger doesn't begin to touch on how I felt right then. Livid, that's a good word. Furious. Outraged. I couldn't believe they refused to pack up Amanda's homework and let me take it to her. I lived with her full-time. I was caring for her while she was sick. Jeff was working long days in Boston and he just wasn't around during school hours.

After some long talks with Jeff about this, I realized that the anger at this injustice was not going away. I recognized it as a powerful energy inside of me, and I instinctively knew that I needed to channel it. As I realized this, I had the idea to start a Stepfamily Support Group. Surely there were other stepparents out there who were going through similar situations and injustices. Maybe we could find a way to get together and at least sympathize with each other. Maybe there would be healing in that.

We put ads for the support group in local newspapers, and people joined us. We shared the angers and frustrations, the joys and losses that we all had in common.

I noticed that as soon as I shared in this group what had happened at Amanda's middle school, my anger slowly and finally dissipated. I never did get her school to give me her homework when she was sick. There was nothing I could do about that. But I was able to recognize my anger and to honor it by allowing its energy to be a force for something good instead of harming myself by ignoring it or harming others by lashing out at them.

Time for Reflection

Look back at your childhood and adolescence. What did you learn about anger from your own family of origin?

Don't judge those people and don't beat yourself up for whatever happened then. If possible, allow your heart to soften and embrace whatever your experience was in the "School of Anger" as you grew up. Allow it to be what it was.

Gather some images of people expressing various stages and shades of anger.

Use one of the images to do some journaling with your own anger. Ask the four basic questions (see link below), or make up some of your own.

You might find it healing to create a SoulCollage® card for your own inner angry Neter. Take a look at my Angry Annie card (see link below) and see if it inspires you in some way.

Honor your anger, or at least one aspect of it, with a SoulCollage® card. Remember, when you create a card for a shadowed part of yourself, you are showing it respect and giving yourself a visual cue to be more aware of it. You are making a commitment to yourself to be in relationship with it and to learn from it, which can only be a good thing!

SoulCollage® Example

Please visit KaleidoSoul.com/into-the-heart-shadow
The password for this page is: shadow

The topic to scroll down to is:
Upside of Anger

SoulCollage® Resource

Visit this page for more information about the I Am the One Who . . . exercise:

kaleidosoul.com/soulcollage-cards-interpreting

CHAPTER 32

Golden Shadow

"GOLDEN SHADOW" REFERS to the *bright* parts of yourself that you have disowned. These are inner voices or personality parts that you might be hiding from for fear of what will happen if you give them space and air in your life.

A recent example from my own life is my inner Theatre Lover. This is a bright and beautiful part of me that I eagerly flirted with in my high school and college years. I played around with her some when I was teaching second grade in the 70's and 80's. Then I shoved her aside for more "serious" things like career and marriage.

From 1995-2005, I was fortunate to work in the box office of a large regional music theater. My inner Theatre Lover was delighted that we landed there. We got to be part of the creative side of theatre productions that we could see *whenever we wanted.* Yes, my theatre lover part was in absolute heaven!

After I left that job, she got put on the back burner again. I locked her away in my inner dungeon. It wasn't a conscious decision. I didn't even think about what this precious part of me might be feeling. I was busy with (you guessed it) more "important" things.

The beauty of SoulCollage® is shown in the fact that after I created a card for her, she appeared in my daily readings from time to time, so I wasn't able to *completely* ignore her. From time to time, I heard her urging me to join a community theatre group and work behind the scenes. I continued to dismiss her with thoughts like, "I don't have time for that," and "There are no theatre groups around here," and "How would I fit into a group like that?"

Finally, my inner Theatre Lover had her way with me. Her voice kept coming to me through the card I'd made for her. Late in 2012, I finally set the intention to find and join a community theatre with the idea of working backstage in some capacity. After a few months of active searching, I was led to a theatre group the next town over, literally five miles from my house! They were mounting a production of *The Sound of Music* and they welcomed me with open arms. I had the time of my life as Props Manager and also earned the title of Assistant Stage Manager. My Theatre Lover was once again in heaven! It was a thoroughly enjoyable, fun adventure, and I feel blessed by the people whose lives touched mine during those five months.

I honestly believe that this whole experience was due to the fact that I had made a card to honor my Theatre Lover, and after a while I simply couldn't ignore her gentle tugging at my sleeve.

Time for Reflection

To help you name some of your own Golden Shadow parts, write the names of three people you admire and look up to as role models. Then list three characteristics of each of these people.

For example:

Thich Nhat Hanh: wise, funny, calm

Katniss Everdeen (heroine from *The Hunger Games*): brave, intelligent, doesn't care what others think

Have fun with this list, and make it longer if you like. You might want to include other characters from television, books, or movies.

The major truth here is that what you admire in others is also a part of you. Otherwise you wouldn't be able to recognize it!

Make an intentional SoulCollage® card for a couple of these characteristics of others that you don't think are part of you. Then listen to them as they tell you more about themselves, and you.

SoulCollage® Example

Please visit KaleidoSoul.com/into-the-heart-shadow
The password for this page is: shadow

The topic to scroll down to is:
Golden Shadow

CHAPTER 33

Life Is Hard . . . Or Is It?

WHEN I WAS growing up, I learned that life is hard work. My father worked two jobs when I was small, just to make ends meet. My mother worked hard at being a homemaker. She cooked and cleaned and looked after my brothers and me. Then she cooked and cleaned some more. When she *did* spend time doing what she loved (writing letters to her pen pals and creating hand-decorated stationery), it was with apology and guilt. Each of my brothers worked their way through college, and I followed in their footsteps. I didn't see people living a life that was grounded in joy. Joy was a frivolous "extra," something talked about only around the holidays, and then never in connection with one's personal life.

As I got older and began my own life, independent of my family of origin, I met some people who had no idea about the "life is hard" philosophy. I was drawn to these people because I wanted what they had. For a long time I struggled with this, because the "life is hard" idea was ingrained so deeply inside of me.

After several years of therapy in my forties, I slowly began to separate from this particular ancestral belief. The freedom I felt was enormous. As I learned to let go of the old adage "life is hard," I found that my life opened up to me in a myriad of wondrous ways.

Once in a while, I do slip back into those old thought patterns and that's okay. My Life is Hard card (see link below) remains in my deck to remind me of what I used to believe. It whispers to me that I no longer need to subscribe to its outdated tenets.

Here's the best part: when I remind myself that life doesn't have to be hard, when I allow the universe to flood my soul with joy, the world doesn't explode and the Guilt Police are nowhere to be found.

Time for Reflection

Can you identify one self-definition that no longer serves you?

What might happen if you let go of this outdated belief?

Make a SoulCollage® card to honor this self-definition. It might take a while to find just the "right" images, so allow the process to unfold for you as it will.

Allow this Neter, this old belief, to tell you its story.

Set an intention to create a new belief in its place. Mine was "I live in a friendly Universe." Create a card for this new belief as well.

SoulCollage® Example

Please visit KaleidoSoul.com/into-the-heart-shadow
The password for this page is: shadow

The topic to scroll down to is:
Life is Hard

CHAPTER 34

The Shadow Knows

ONCE YOU STARTED doing SoulCollage®, it probably wasn't long before you came face to face with a couple of images that represented a part of yourself you didn't like. For me, that part was my Inner Critic, whom I lovingly refer to as Ethel.

After reading a lot about our inner shadows, talking with Seena about it, and attending a workshop on this topic, I learned something magnificent that really changed my life. A huge shift took place when I realized that *I wasn't supposed to change or fix any of these shadowed parts but simply accept them as they are and assist them in coming to balance.*

Now, say this out loud to yourself right now:

I am not supposed to change or fix any of my shadowed parts. I can simply accept them as they are and then consider how to bring them to balance.

Ah, yes. Do you feel a shift inside of you when you say that to yourself? It's a very powerful concept to assimilate into our lives. Let's explore it a bit further.

Seena likes to express it like this: each part of us has a *positive intent* and a *negative potential.* In other words, each Neter has an intention that is a gift to us as well as a potential to be destructive.

Here's an example. I'd been aware for some time of my Inner Critic's harsh running commentary. After starting SoulCollage® and making a card for her, I became even more aware of her.

Soon after that, an old family friend suffering from fibromyalgia came to visit us from California for three months. Given the amount of pain she was in, Lynne was very needy. We'd been friends since second grade, so I loved her and wanted to take care of her. However, I also had a business to run and other family obligations to take care of. During the first month of Lynne's stay with us, I became even more aware of my Inner Critic, Ethel. If I spent the day with Lynne, Ethel would start nattering away at me that I was ruining my business. If I spent the day working in my study, Ethel would be shouting at me that I was being a bad friend to Lynne.

Because I was doing a lot of journaling then, I began to see exactly what was happening. I realized that there was no satisfying Ethel! I was damned if I did one thing and damned if I did the opposite. I couldn't win, no matter what. As long as I was listening to Ethel and buying into her ever-changing story, I was going to be miserable and unproductive. At that point I realized that I could hear what she was telling me, but I didn't have to buy into it. *I didn't have to believe her.*

That's when I decided to spend some "quality time" with my Inner Critic, offering acceptance. I sat down with my Ethel card and my journal. "What is your *positive intent* for me?" I asked. "Who are you when you are in balance?"

The answer, after a bit of journaling, came right out. Ethel told me that her real role in my life is that of Truth Teller. It's only when I push her away and ignore her that she flips into shaming criticism to get my attention. That's her *negative potential.*

It takes time to discern the positive intent of a shadowed part as well as to clarify the negative potential of a brighter part. You might ask a shadowed Neter to tell you its positive intent but it might not be ready to tell you. Try holding that question in your mind for a few weeks or months (or longer) until one day the answer becomes clear.

One of the biggest gifts that SoulCollage® gives us is this ability to see the gifts in our shadows. There is great freedom when we realize that we don't have to fix or change these troublesome parts, only to accept them and bring them back to balance.

Time for Reflection

Choose one of your own shadowed parts. Make a card for it if you haven't already.

Journal with it. Allow it to tell you its story. Let it pour out its feelings. Don't judge this part of you. Just accept it. Offer it compassion and kindness if you can.

Then ask it "What is your positive intent for me?" or "Who are you when you are in balance?" Let it respond.

Practice offering acceptance to your shadowed parts as they show up. See if you experience a shift in your life.

SoulCollage® Example

Please visit KaleidoSoul.com/into-the-heart-shadow
The password for this page is: shadow

The topic to scroll down to is:
Shadow Knows

Council Suit

Overview

The Council Suit represents the archetypal dimension, or the "larger story" of our lives. Seena Frost, founder of SoulCollage®, describes archetypes as "the invisible guides, challengers, creators and destroyers, known across time and cultures by many names, yet being somehow universally in the collective unconscious of the human race."

Archetypes are seen as recurring images and figures in art, literature, religion, myth, and film, with no regard to culture or time. I like to think of archetypes as "Capital-Letter-Energies." For example: Warrior - not the man who goes to fight for his country, but the theme or *idea* of Warrior which is found in any time, any place, any culture, any religion. Other examples might be: Caretaker, Lover, Wise Woman, Hermit, Seeker, Mother, and Teacher. There are many more. In this way, we can define archetypes as motifs, themes, or ancient patterns.

The essays in this section focus on several archetypes that have influenced me throughout my life. You may relate to these; you may not. The important thing to remember is that archetypes choose us, not the other way around!

More information about the Council Suit can be found here: KaleidoSoul.com/archetypes

CHAPTER 35

Time and Time Again

I HAVE A card in my deck called Time in a Bottle (see link below). Remember the Jim Croce song from the 70's? My card, like his song, accurately reflects exactly how I feel about the passing of time. Sometimes I look at the card and think that the large image of the woman in the top right corner might be the Keeper of Time, but whenever I read from it, I always tap into the sad, frustrated energy of time passing.

> *I Am the One Who is running out of time. I Am the One Who knows that I don't have all the time in the world. I Am the One Who is afraid that I won't get everything done in time.*
>
> *I Am the One Who has so much to share with the world and not enough time to do it all. I Am the One Who tries to capture time and save it, hoard it, hang on to it because I think I can control it better this way.*
>
> *My message for you today is this: Pay attention to your relationship with time. You are hurting yourself with your attitude towards time. Time keeps ticking on, even if you hoard all of the clocks in the world into locked jars and cabinets.*

Whenever I draw this card in a reading, it seems to come at times when there are more than the usual items on my To-Do Lists, when I can't quite seem to catch up. Even so, I find great comfort in this card, even though it seems to remind me of my powerlessness in the face of Time. It helps me to remember that time is just a mental construct, and all that matters is that I continue to keep myself in *this* moment, right now. When I stay in the present moment, then I find deep peace, and my worries and fears about getting everything done simply fade away.

I recently read a creative prompt online that suggested we create a piece of art for our Time Muse. This really resonated with me so I made a SoulCollage® card for my own Time Muse (see link below). Here are the wise words she has for me today:

I Am the One Who is peaceful and content in this moment. I Am the One Who takes my time and moves slowly, absorbing everything I see and hear and feel. I Am the One Who knows that there is only One Moment - this one, right here, right now.

My message for you today is this: Earlier, you mentioned a Keeper of Time. I am here to tell you that Time is not "kept." It is spent, enjoyed, savored. You cannot "keep" time or "waste" time; you can only BE in relation to time. So slow down, keep still, close your eyes, breathe deeply, and savor the only time you have - this present moment.

Time for Reflection

Do you have a card in your deck that gives image to the theme of Time or your relationship with it? If so, do some journaling with this Neter. What wisdom does it have to give you about Time right now in your life?

If you don't have a card like this, seek out some images and make a card.

Read the words from my Time Muse again. What do you think and feel about the fact that Time cannot be kept, even though we dizzy ourselves trying? Journal with this idea and see what comes up for you.

Do a three-card reading with your deck as you ask the question, "Who has wisdom to give me about my relationship with Time?" or "How can I relax into the essence of Time in this present moment?" If neither of these questions feels right to you, create your own.

SoulCollage® Example

Please visit KaleidoSoul.com/into-the-heart-council
The password for this page is: pattern

The topic to scroll down to is:
Time

SoulCollage® Example

Visit this page for more information about doing a three-card reading:
kaleidosoul.com/cardreadings

CHAPTER 36

Peaceful Warrior Rides Again

AT A RECENT SoulCollage® gathering, I found myself in a discussion about the current political situation in the United States. The topic of archetypes came up and someone referred to the battle between the two current presidential candidates as a contest between a Warrior and a Peacemaker.

Since SoulCollage® does not play favorites when it comes to politics or religion, I won't go into which presidential candidate was being governed by which archetype. I only mention it here as a reminder that everyone around us (well-known or otherwise) is influenced by ancient archetypes.

I also mention it because it reminded me that in my own personal Council of archetypes, I don't have a Warrior *or* a Peacemaker. Instead, I have a Peaceful Warrior (see link below).

She came to me very early in my own SoulCollage® journey. I made the card intuitively, and when I initially journaled with this Neter, I was surprised to hear her telling me that she is my Peaceful Warrior. I hadn't been consciously aware of her before, but listening to her and looking back on my life I can see the kernel of truth that she shares with me. I have never been one to valiantly charge in to save the day, or rescue someone with clanging symbols and loud bellows. *My* Warrior's way is softer, gentler, and more low-key. She handles conflict peacefully.

Several months after meeting Peaceful Warrior within this card, I was in a difficult situation where I worked. There had been a huge mis-understanding over something I had said about my boss, and I found myself being reprimanded unfairly by *her* boss. In the midst of my anger, I did a SoulCollage® reading for guidance, and Peaceful Warrior is one of the two cards that I randomly drew.

I did some journaling with her, and she told me that I could rely on her energy and strength to deal with this situation. She gave me the idea to talk this out in a reasonable and peaceful manner with David, my boss's boss. I realized that I could stand up for myself in a real and visible way while utilizing this Peaceful Warrior energy to calm the rough waters. I actually propped the card up on my desk beside the phone when I called David the next day. This Neter's strong yet peaceful energy enabled me to stand my ground in a way that wasn't hurtful to anyone, while expressing myself in a way that allowed each of us to be heard and understood.

It was a powerful experience that I will never forget. Not just the phone call itself, but the fact that I went to my deck with a real need, and received an immediate, practical, wise answer.

Time for Reflection

Take some time this week to think about the archetypes of Warrior, Peacemaker, and Peaceful Warrior in your own world. How do these themes play out in people and places that you know? Do you relate more strongly to one or another? What are the bright and shadowed sides of each of these archetypes?

If you resonate with one of these archetypes more strongly than another, look for images that you can relate to and create a card for it for your own deck.

SoulCollage® Examples

Please visit KaleidoSoul.com/into-the-heart-council
The password for this page is: pattern

The topic to scroll down to is:
Warrior

SoulCollage® Resource

Visit this page for more information about doing a card reading:

kaleidosoul.com/cardreadings

CHAPTER 37

Fire-Tending

WHEN I WAS 10 years old, the house next door burned completely to the ground. We were woken up at 3 a.m. by the sound of blaring sirens. All the families on our street were kept awake for hours by the acrid smell of smoke, the sharp snapping of the flames, and the shouts of dozens of firemen.

It was a scary night for everyone, including me, who up until that point had only seen fire as something "pretty." My previous experience with fire had been limited to pristine white candles on the altar at church and slim green tapers in a holiday centerpiece. The idea that a single flame could burgeon out of control and destroy so much had never entered my young mind.

A few years later I joined the Girl Scouts and spent many a happy evening sitting around campfires, singing songs, toasting marshmallows, and savoring the warmth of the lingering flames. We built fires for heating water and cooking our food on many a camping trip. I was learning that fire could be harnessed and used for good; that it wasn't just destructive. Precautions could be taken.

Looking back on my relationship with fire over the years, I can see that I've grown and changed right along with my learning about this element. Yes, fire can be *pretty*. It can also be *destructive*. At the same time, it can be *useful*. I understand now that it's all a matter of balance. A campfire can be beautiful, and it can serve us in many ways, but if we don't tend it carefully, we run the risk of unleashing fire's destructiveness.

This is true of so many things in our lives. Each inner Committee part can be helpful and uplifting, as long as we pay attention to it, as long as we give it space and room. However, as soon as we start ignoring it or treating it badly in some way, it can turn shadowy, fierce, even destructive.

Take a look at my SoulCollage® card for the archetypal theme of Passion (see link below). I made this card intuitively, not knowing why I was putting these images together. Someone who saw it then told me it reminded them of the Hawaiian goddess Pele. In addition to being recognized as the goddess of fire, lightning, and volcanoes, Pele is also known for her creative power, passion, purpose, and profound love. When the figure on this card spoke to me, she said:

> *I Am the One Who lifts my arms to Spirit. I Am the One with passion and fire for my life, my heart, my wholeness. I am Fire Dancer. I am the passion that guides you. I am bright and burning and hot. I Am the One Who burns away the impurities in your life.*
>
> The wisdom she had to give me was this: *Do not bury your passions, Dear One. Bring them to the surface. Let them simmer and burn through your body, your mind, your spirit, and your life. Let your passions proclaim your unique self to the world!*

This Neter led me to take an in-depth look at what my passions really were at that time in my life. She opened my heart to the awareness that passions well-tended, like well-tended flames, can burn hot and wild without destroying.

Time for Reflection

What are you passionate about right now? What dreams and ideas are burning brightly in your heart?

Take care to tend these passions. Give them air this week, and always.

Pay attention to your passions. You are the one responsible for seeing that they don't burn out.

Make a SoulCollage® card for the archetypal energy of Passion or Fire. Pay attention to the gifts this Neter is offering to you.

Do a random reading with your deck after asking this question: "Which Neters have wisdom to give me about tending my passions?"

SoulCollage® Example

Please visit KaleidoSoul.com/into-the-heart-council
The password for this page is: pattern

The topic to scroll down to is:
Passion

SoulCollage® Resource

Visit this page for more information about doing a random card reading:
kaleidosoul.com/cardreadings

CHAPTER 38

Angel of Sorrow

THERE IS A powerful card in my deck (see link below) that I made intuitively many years ago, thinking that it was about the inner part of me who grieves when I experience sadness and loss. At least, that is what was going through my mind as I was selecting images and gluing them down on the card.

I didn't work with this card right away. I placed it in my deck and it didn't show up in a reading until a year later when I was grieving the loss of our dear cat Scooter. He was 12 years old, a proud hunter, and his soul lived for the great outdoors. He was also a big baby who loved to sleep on our bed, nap on the catnip blanket, and beg for tuna treats in the kitchen. After Scooter was gone, we still had two cats in our feline family, but he had left an empty place in our hearts that was only his to fill.

I was fairly new to SoulCollage® when Scooter died. At first I couldn't quite grasp how SoulCollage® could help me through this heartbreak. I didn't think SoulCollage® was actually big enough to hold this deep hollow ache inside of me. Then I happened to draw the card that I mentioned above, in a SoulCollage® reading. After dialoging with it, I discovered that SoulCollage® most definitely *is* wide and spacious enough to include even the deepest sorrow.

Here is what this Neter said to me:

I Am the One Who grieves with you when you hear bad news or when you suffer in any way. I Am the One Who feels your losses as deeply as you do. I Am the One Who honors your loss, who holds your loss, who allows you to grieve.

I Am the One Who sits with you in the shadows of your pain and vulnerability. I Am the One Who breathes new life into you when your grieving is done. I Am the One Who walks hand in hand with Sorrow. I Am the One Who helps you to bear the pain of your loss.

I give you acceptance and hope. I give you new directions, new life. I give you the knowledge that you are not alone, that you don't have to bear any of it alone.

I want you to feel the pain of your grieving. I want you to enter it fully and to hold my hand when you are in that space. I want you to know that sorrow has its own gifts, and you cannot receive them until you enter that particular darkness. I want to you know that the darkness of your grief is safe when you invite me to join you in that darkness.

I had thought that this card was about the *inner* Committee part of me who grieves, but it spoke to me from a place *outside* of me instead. This Neter is now known to me as Angel of Sorrow. She has appeared often in my card readings to offer comfort as well as permission to fully grieve any loss or heartache I may be experiencing.

Time for Reflection:

Pause for a moment right now and step back from your life, observing it as if you were a stranger. Is Grief knocking at the door of your soul today? Are you losing or have you recently lost someone or something dear to you? Are you experiencing a more subtle loss, a transition of some kind that involves letting go of the old to make room for the new? Is there a loss from your past that you pushed aside and never fully grieved?

Make a list of ways you can comfort and take care of yourself as you allow yourself the experience of this loss, however old or new it is.

Include SoulCollage® in some way on your list. You could make a card or do a reading. You might choose to create your own Angel of Sorrow card to remind you that you are not alone when you grieve.

SoulCollage® Example

Please visit KaleidoSoul.com/into-the-heart-council
The password for this page is: pattern

The topic to scroll down to is:
Sorrow

CHAPTER 39

The Rainy Season

EVER HEAR THE expression *Rain, rain, go away, come again another day?* Well, it took on new meaning here in Massachusetts a while ago when it rained for ten days straight! We had a few days respite, and then we got some more! I was at the dentist's office a few days after the second deluge and overheard the receptionist talking with another patient about gardening.

"I wish the sun would come out," the patient groaned. "I've got so many plants just sitting on my porch, waiting to go in the ground."

"Don't worry about it," said the receptionist. "The ground is perfect for planting right now. All you need to do is dig a hole and plop 'em in!"

We all laughed, but she was absolutely right. Even I (the only one in my family born *without* the proverbial green thumb) was able to quickly and easily "plop" in some perennials that week. Why? Because the soil was so soft, prepared, and ready. Soft, prepared, and made ready by many dreary, rainy days.

During that time, I was struggling with my own sadness and grief over the loss of our beloved cat, Scooter. Some days I thought that my tears would go on forever, but I allowed myself those tears, and I allowed the discomfort that comes with such deep sorrow.

As I allowed my grief space and time, I learned something powerful. If so much rain makes the soil fertile and easy for planting, then it follows that so much sorrow and grief can make the ground of our souls lush and ready for new seeds.

I made a Council card several months ago. I call her the Cosmic Gardener (see link below). I made this card intuitively and when I journaled with her, this is what she said to me:

I Am the One Who tends to all growing things. I Am the One Who kneels in prayer and gratitude as I watch things and people grow. I Am the One Who shelters growing things in the light. I give you as much inner growth as your mind and soul and body are ready for. I give you strength in your growth, gratitude for your growth, peace and light in your growth.

I made this card before we got hit with all that rain, months before my heart was deluged with so much sorrow, but her lessons are coming clear to me more and more, now that the sun is back to shining on a regular basis again (on the earth *and* in my soul).

Time for Reflection

Think back to a time in your life when your own heart and soul were flooded with sadness for too many days. Did you allow yourself the rainy season? If not, why not?

Looking at your life now, can you see any new seeds that flourished in the aftermath of that soul rain?

Make a SoulCollage® card for your own Cosmic Gardener, the one who oversees all growth.

SoulCollage® Example

Please visit KaleidoSoul.com/into-the-heart-council
The password for this page is: pattern

The topic to scroll down to is:
Growth

CHAPTER 40

In My Dreams

SEENA FROST TEACHES that archetypes are guides on our journey; each one brings a task, a lesson, and a gift, as well as liabilities (shadow). I once heard her say that if we *ignore* our archetypes, they cannot help us, but if we are open to them, their gifts are easier to see.

For me, Teacher is a predominant archetype that has been with me since I was a little girl playing "school" with the neighborhood kids. I was able to honor this archetype's gifts by studying elementary education in college and was delighted beyond belief when I was given my own second grade classroom in Amelia, Virginia, when I was 22.

I left Amelia after six years for a job as an educational consultant for a computer learning company. I found myself once again in the throes of Teacher energy as I taught teachers and administrators as well as children of many ages.

In 1992 I gave up teaching to help my husband raise his children from his first marriage. I held several odd jobs during the years that followed, including bookstore clerk and customer service representative at a music theatre. Teaching did not play a role in my life for over 10 years.

Now here's something interesting. Every September during those non-teaching years, I would have vivid dreams about teaching. In the dreams I would find myself back in the classroom, experiencing the thrill of greeting a new class of students, savoring the blessing of creating and passing on lessons. These dreams puzzled me because I was burned out from teaching in a public school system and I honestly did not want to go back to the classroom.

But guess what? In 2005, when I started teaching SoulCollage® classes, those teaching dreams stopped completely and I've never had another one since! It wasn't until a few years later when I was learning about archetypes via the SoulCollage® process, that I realized I wasn't *dreaming* about teaching any more because I was *teaching*. There was simply no need for this archetypal energy to be tapping me on my sleepy shoulder any longer!

The lesson here is to be aware of any archetypes who might be showing up in your dreams. They are guides and they are there to help you. The more aware of them you are, the more gifts they can give.

Time for Reflection

Close your eyes and think of one archetypal energy that has been with you since childhood.

If you don't have a card for this archetype yet, seek out some images and set an intention to make one.

How is this archetype showing up in your life today? If its energy is absent, invite it into your dreams and see who or what shows up!

CHAPTER 41

The Ancient Pattern of Story

WHEN I WAS first learning about archetypes at the beginning of my SoulCollage® journey ten years ago, I knew immediately that Story is an archetypal energy that has had a strong hold on me since I was very young. My parents read stories to me from a very young age, and then I learned to read them myself. I began writing my own stories as early as the second grade, and as I grew older, I gave in to the pleasure of creating plays and novels. Looking back, I can see how stories that were told in television shows, movies, books, and songs throughout the years have touched and deepened my own life.

Carolyn Myss refers to archetypes as "ancient patterns that exist in human consciousness." Sit and breathe with this phrase for a moment. Ancient patterns. Existing in human consciousness. For me, Story is indeed an ancient pattern that is known throughout all human existence, no matter what one's race, creed or culture.

I couldn't find anything in any research I did about Capital-S-Story being an archetype. But I had listened well to Seena Frost. There are many archetypal energies that aren't listed in the popular books available on this topic. We each know our own life so much better than any other, so I made a card to honor this idea, this theme of Story that has prevailed throughout my life (see link below to take a peek at my card). Here is what this Neter says to me:

I Am the One Who offers the gift of light through the power of Story. I Am the One Who gives the story words and meaning. I Am the One Who creates the story, who enables you to see the story in many different ways. I Am the One Who teaches and gets messages across through stories. I

Am the One Who gifts and inspires your inner writer. I Am the One Who fosters your love of reading, your love of television, your love of movies.

My message for you today is this: I am a huge part of your life. My energy has been active inside of you from the very beginning and will continue to the end. Pay attention to me. Honor me by allowing my energy to flow through you especially through your writing.

Time for Reflection

Do you relate to this theme of Story in your own life? How and when has it played an integral part in your journey? Gather some images to honor this archetype with a card.

If you don't relate to this particular archetype, meditate this week on the idea of archetypes as ancient patterns that exist in human consciousness. Looking back over your life with this in mind, what patterns do you notice? Choose an archetypal energy that you want to honor with a SoulCollage® card and commit to making it within the month if you can find the "right" images.

SoulCollage® Example

Please visit KaleidoSoul.com/into-the-heart-council
The password for this page is: pattern

The topic to scroll down to is:
Story

Seasons and Holidays

Overview

The four seasons have much to teach us about the cycles of our own lives. I look upon the seasonal energies of Spring, Summer, Autumn, and Winter as archetypes that play out again and again in a myriad of ways in my life.

This section contains essays on relating SoulCollage® to the four seasons, as well as various holidays such as Valentine's Day and those sometimes stressful celebration days that occur in the month of December.

CHAPTER 42

Spring: The Blossom Rule

HERE IN NEW England, it feels like winter lasted a lot longer than usual this year. Perhaps I notice it more because I'm getting "older." Or maybe I am more aware of the turning of the seasons because of the daily walks I take with our dog Suzy.

It was easy to ignore what was happening outdoors when I could stay inside if I felt like it. But braving the elements *every* day, no matter what, has made it hard to disregard the harshness of winter. I have been acutely aware of the cold air, the frozen trees, the icy sidewalks. As the days and weeks and months went on, I became more and more aware of a deep yearning inside of me for warmth, flowers, and spring.

As it is with everything in life, the longer the period of bleakness, the more grateful we are when it ends. Because this winter was especially long and dreary, I feel much more joy when I see a sweet crocus breaking through the dirt or a burst of bright yellow forsythia around the corner. Because we just spent almost six months in long johns, sweatpants, and heavy woolen turtlenecks, it is much more glorious to be able to walk outside in short sleeves and feel the warm sun caress our bare arms.

I am reminded of a beautiful lily plant that I brought home many years ago. The buds on the plant were closed tightly when I set it on my kitchen table. I knew in my head that if I kept it warm and gave it water to drink, the buds would open to full blossom. But still, I found myself worrying that this plant would be the exception to the "blossom rule." I was afraid that the buds would never open, that the time of fragrant opening would never happen.

I was much younger then. I had not weathered many winter storms. Indeed, those lily buds opened their beauty to me. Of course they did. That is the rule of blossoming. Buds burst open with warmth and water and sunlight. They just do. The power of growth is too great to keep them closed forever.

It is the knowing of this "Blossom Rule" that gets me through our long New England winters. When I don't think I can take another icy day, I simply give my thought and energy to the bulbs that lay dormant under the frozen dirt of our snow-laden garden. I remind myself that winters do *not* last forever. The Blossom Rule is *always* and *forever* true.

Time for Reflection

Do you believe in the "Blossom Rule?"

What is blossoming in your own life right now? How can you nurture this new growth?

If you are drawn to the archetypal energy of Spring, make a SoulCollage® card to honor it in your deck.

SoulCollage® Example

Please visit KaleidoSoul.com/into-the-heart-seasons
The password for this page is: change

The topic to scroll down to is:
Spring

CHAPTER 43

Sweet Summertime

AFTER THE GROWTH-FILLED season of Spring, the earth transitions into the heat of summer. Nature's cycle reaches its zenith as all growing things come to fullness in the light and warmth of the sun. Luxurious growth is everywhere. Plants and flowers, fruits and vegetables reach maturity and find full expression.

My SoulCollage® card for the season of Summer came to me accidentally. No, not accidentally. It came to me *intuitively*. I had made cards for the other seasons and was seeking images for a Summer card. One day I did a reading with my deck and a card that had previously been a mystery to me revealed itself as representing the archetypal energy of Summer.

You can see my card at the link below. Here is what she said to me:

> *I Am the One Who is female and standing in lush greenery and golden light. I Am the One Who is surrounded by flowers and growing things that are in full bloom. I am the one who smiles at the juiciness of life that is all around me. I am the one who is Summer at its fullest, most glorious expression.*

SoulCollage® Example

Please visit KaleidoSoul.com/into-the-heart-seasons
The password for this page is: change

The topic to scroll down to is:
Summer

CHAPTER 44

Autumn Transformation

EVER SINCE I was a little girl, I have been drawn to the season of Autumn. At first it was just about the magic of the leaves changing colors. I live in New England where I never cease to be thrilled when the lush greenery of summer turns to the bright palette of earthy Autumn.

When I discovered that leaves change colors due to the lack of chlorophyll because they are actually *dying*, I was dismayed at first. That seemed a harsh lesson in reality for a mere 10-year-old! But as I got older, I realized that this is all a part of the tremendously beautiful life cycle we are all gifted with. Birth. Growth. Life. Death. It's all entwined. Without the dying leaves and the starkness of winter, there can be spring, no summer, no growth.

As I've grown, I have come to love the season of Autumn for reasons that go beyond the crimson, orange, and deep ginger-colored leaves that crunch under my feet on my brisk morning walks. For me, autumn is also a time for *harvesting* and *composting*.

As the air I breathe turns crisp with hints of winter's chill, and as the nights begin to get longer, I find myself beginning to move inward, rooting around inside myself for a warm place to "land." I feel myself thinking about the year I've just lived, going back over my activities of Winter, Spring, and Summer. What have I harvested? What will I take with me into the coming season of Winter? What needs to be turned over and composted for the richness of my inner life?

There was a wonderful scene in a recent episode of *The Middle*, a realistic little American sitcom that I am quite fond of. A seven-year-old boy named Brick has been given the task of raking up all of the leaves in his family's yard. It takes him a week, but he does it with pride and joy. When he is done and he finds out that his father is going to *burn* the leaves, Brick is heartbroken. "Can't we just take them to the forest and let them go?" he says through his tears. At first his father laughs at him. After all, they are "just leaves." But in the end, father and son take the bags of leaves to the forest and indeed, they let them go.

Time for Reflection

What have you harvested from the previous months that you want to take with you into the next cycle of seasons?

What do you need to let go of? What do you want to let go of?

If you are drawn to the archetype of Autumn, make a SoulCollage® card for it and allow it to speak to you of change and transformation.

SoulCollage® Example

Please visit KaleidoSoul.com/into-the-heart-seasons
The password for this page is: change

The topic to scroll down to is:
Autumn

CHAPTER 45

Searching for a Perfect Leaf

IT'S THE HEART of Autumn right now in New England, a beautiful season of bright colors, cool crisp air, and abundant harvest. Go to your computer now and take a look at the beautiful photo taken by my niece, Stephanie Pacheco, who lives in Vermont (see link below). Gaze at it for a moment. Take in the brilliant tapestry of variegated color and soulful beauty. Breathe it in . . . and then breathe out any anxiety that is floating around in your mind today.

The colors in this image are made up of hundreds of thousands of leaves. You can't see each one individually here, but you know in your mind that they exist, and that together they create this beautiful vista for us to appreciate and admire. This brings to mind a story I read recently in the book *Healing Words* by Larry Dossey. A woman told the author of a game she played with her friends when she was little. The game was called "Find a Perfect Leaf." For hours on end, they would sort and sift through the piles of leaves in their backyards and on the lawns of their neighbors, looking for one perfect leaf. Most days they all came up empty-handed, because when it comes to leaves, there really is no such thing.

I was intrigued by this concept, so for the past few weeks on my morning walks, I've been picking up leaves that seem "perfect," only to find that they are not. A tiny hole here, a ripped edge there. Unseemly veins, marred stems, blemishes. It seems that no matter how perfect a leaf seems from a distance, when you get a close-up look at it, imperfection claims it in some way, large or small.

Instead of being disappointed by all the flawed leaves out there, I was reminded that the same thing is true of humans too. Not one of us is perfect, even though we spend a great deal of our lives trying to be. It saves me a lot of time and energy if I can remember this.

If I can be as gentle with my own imperfections as I am with the marred spots and torn edges of the leaves that grace my morning walks, then I leave myself more open to accepting the beauty that is all around me, every moment, every day. This is as true of lovely Autumn leaves as it is of my own beautiful family and friends, and especially myself!

Time for Reflection

Take another look at the photograph in the link below. Breathe with it for a few moments again, remembering that thousands and thousands of imperfect leaves make up that vista.

Breathe in the beauty . . . then breathe out any of your own imperfections that have caused you to be less than kind to yourself. Breathe in the collective beauty of those leaves . . . then breathe out any imperfections of your loved ones that have caused you to be less than loving towards them.

Make a list of some of your own imperfections. Try to do this without judgment. You are simply observing yourself: "Hmm . . . this is interesting." If it gets overwhelming, make a separate list of things that you love about yourself.

Do you have SoulCollage® cards for any of these imperfect parts of yourself? See if you can find some images to let these inner parts have a voice, and invite them to tell you their story.

You might want to make a card for your inner Perfectionist or for the part of you who actually is comfortable with your own imperfections.

Photo Example

Please visit KaleidoSoul.com/into-the-heart-seasons
The password for this page is: change

The topic to scroll down to is:
Perfect Leaf

CHAPTER 46

Living Within My Harvest

IT WAS ONE of those serendipitous moments which happened, strangely enough, in a discount department store that happened to be right next to the movie theatre I was heading towards. I had a little time before my movie started so I bopped in to have a look around. I don't usually browse these stores for clothing; I'm more apt to find something interesting for our house, or something seasonally decorative for an upcoming SoulCollage® retreat or workshop.

After several minutes of enjoyable shopping . . . Bam! There it was, a framed piece of simple embroidery in the stark colors of Autumn: brown, cream, black, tan, orange (see link below). A bare tree, scattered with crows and some leaves drifting lazily to the ground. These words were at the bottom: *Live Within Your Harvest*. Whoa! I was stunned by the simple power of this, and as often happens with imagery, it went straight to my heart and soul.

It was a one-of-a-kind piece. At first I was disappointed because my first response was to buy as many as I could to give away as gifts. But then I began to think of it differently: *maybe this is a gift, meant just for me today*. So I purchased it, lovingly carried it home and propped it up on the altar in my Quiet Room where I've been walking by it reverently ever since.

Time for Reflection

What exactly is your harvest? What does it mean to live *within* your harvest? How are you doing that right now? If you're not doing that right now, how can you begin?

What seeds did you plant several months ago that have grown rich and full? Which seeds did you plant that haven't sprouted yet? Can you accept the fact that some seeds have sprouted, and some have not?

What do you need to gather into your spiritual barn this month in order to be more ready for the darkness of the long winter months?

What would a SoulCollage® card called "Living Within My Harvest" look like? If you want to make one, start gathering images now and create one when the time feels right.

SoulCollage® Example

Please visit KaleidoSoul.com/into-the-heart-seasons
The password for this page is: change

The topic to scroll down to is:
Harvest

CHAPTER 47

Winter Gifts Beneath the Surface

I AM WRITING this in the midst of *yet another* New England snowstorm. The sky is a heavy, steely gray and the snow pours down all thick and blowy. I can see individual snowflakes as they fall; they are large and wet and wild. More than two feet of snow blanket the ground here already and I expect that when this blizzard is over there will be almost three feet of it layered in our yard.

One of my stepdaughters is going through a challenging time right now and recently we were reminiscing about the happy summer hours spent with her children in our back yard: splashing in the kiddie pool, digging in the sandbox, wearing nothing but bathing suits, chasing the dog in the hot sun.

I look out the window now and those memories of warmer times seem really hard to grasp. There is no space now for laughing in the sun, or warmth, or green grass. All is frozen. All is dark. All is still.

And yet.

What about the tulip, daffodil, and crocus bulbs that we planted in November before the first frost? Are they never going to grace our front walkway with color? What about the cherry tree that sits covered in wet snow in the middle of our front lawn? Will it never bloom again? What about the crickets that sing to us softly on warm spring evenings? Are they gone forever?

I offer a loud "of course not" to all three questions! In spite of this harsh winter weather, it is vitally important to remember that there is growth happening beneath the surface. There is movement, however slight, in the bulbs beneath the earth, in the roots of the tree which seem frozen in the winter's harsh darkness, in the absence of the call of the crickets in the woods.

The bulbs that I planted in the fall, the cherry tree that blooms so beautifully in the spring, and the crickets that serenade us all summer . . . we cannot see them right now in the midst of the harsh winter cold, but they are still there, doing their work underground, their beautiful hidden work, guided by Spirit underneath the frozen soil.

So too, even in the midst of a wintery season in our own lives, there is growth happening, just below the surface. My stepdaughter's life right now feels like her own personal winter, like nothing good will ever happen again in her life. She feels at a dead end, heartbroken and weary, bent over with the weight of sadness, like the barren trees in our front yard that are bowed over with the burden of the snow. She cannot see or even think about the fact that life operates in cyclical movements, that nothing is static, that everything changes. She is stuck in the harsh reality of her own winter.

She is young, but I have been through many winters in my life, and I have learned that sooner or later, the sun comes back out, the snow melts, the days get longer. Because of the certainty of the seasons, I know that her sadness will lift, infinitesimally at first, then enough so that she can breathe more easily and see more clearly the little joys that pop up in her life like crocuses in the first light of spring. I also know that she will emerge from this Winter season stronger, wiser, and more deeply rooted in her own being, because I know that there is growth happening even though she cannot see it right now through the severe blizzard that has stormed through her life.

Time for Reflection

Spend some time journaling about those times in your life when you thought you would never be able to dig out of the sadness, the darkness, the cold. What have you learned from the Winter seasons of your own life? What gifts has Winter given you?

What is growing under the layers of frozen snow in your own life? Can you sense the movement of growth in the stillness? If you can't sense the growth, can you have faith that it is there?

If you are drawn to the archetype of Winter, make a SoulCollage® card to honor it in your deck and allow it to speak to you of the gifts beneath the surface.

SoulCollage® Example

Please visit KaleidoSoul.com/into-the-heart-seasons
The password for this page is: change

The topic to scroll down to is:
Winter

CHAPTER 48

Light Up Your Holidays

EARLY ON MY journey with SoulCollage®, I created a card (see link below) to honor my own feelings about "the holidays." It has served me every year since, as it has a special place near our family Christmas tree.* This card reminds me of what I value and treasure the most about the holidays: light, warmth, joy, tradition, giving, and magic.

Your list might be different, and that's perfectly okay. It's a matter of taking a look at your own view of the holidays and deciding what takes priority for you this particular year.

It's so easy to get caught up in the frenzy of shopping and buying "perfect" gifts and baking dozens of cookies and trying to attend every holiday party. I have been there, done that, and it just doesn't "do it" for me anymore! After making this SoulCollage® card, I can see very clearly that I want my holidays to be about *being* rather than *doing*.

So to light up my own holidays, I am seeking out ways to bring *light*, *joy*, *tradition*, and *magic* to this month while honoring my need to simply *be*. It's a tricky balance to maintain, for sure, but it can be done.

Also, in seeking to honor these values throughout December, I try to pay careful attention to what is going on inside of me at any given moment. For example, Perfectionista, and Ethel (my Inner Critic), tend to get out of control during this season. If I am holding myself to the holidays that my mother used to create for us, then each of those inner voices have a lot to say about how I'm falling short, and this can drive me to distraction. Julianna, my Inner Child, tends to act out by overeating and compulsive shopping if I stop paying attention to her in the hustle and bustle of the season.

As long as I am aware of these Neters and what they are saying to me at any given moment, I find it much easier to remain true to my own spirit as reflected in my SoulCollage® card. At any time, I can bring forward other, brighter Neters to dialogue with Ethel, Perfectionista, and Julianna. These other Neters who are helpful to access during the holiday season (for me) are: Magical Child, Yogini, Going with the Flow, Mother Love, and Pausing.

 * Please note that although I personally celebrate Christmas, your holidays might include Hanukkah, Kwanza, Solstice, or something else entirely. The idea here is to honor and celebrate whatever this holiday season means to *you*.

Time for Reflection

Gather some images that reflect the energy of what you want your holidays to look like this year. Create a SoulCollage® card with some of these images. Remember, it doesn't have to be perfect! If you don't have time to make a new card, gather some images and place them where you can see them every day as you get ready for the holidays.

 Do some journaling with your image or card. Ask it the four basic questions. Listen to what this Neter tells you.

 Do a card reading where you draw three cards randomly from your deck, asking this question: *Who has wisdom to give me about how I can bring more joy and light into the upcoming holidays?* Allow the three cards you've drawn to answer your question.

SoulCollage® Example

Please visit KaleidoSoul.com/into-the-heart-seasons
The password for this page is: change

The topic to scroll down to is:
Holidays

SoulCollage® Resource

Visit this page for more information about the four basic questions:
kaleidosoul.com/soulcollage-cards-interpreting

Visit this page for more information about doing a card reading:
kaleidosoul.com/cardreadings

CHAPTER 49

Do-Be Do-Be Do-Be Do

GABRIELLA, MY INNER overachiever, is always extra active during the holidays. For some reason, December brings out her passion for To-Do lists! Believe me when I tell you that she has been creating lists upon lists these past few weeks. I currently have To-Do lists for:

- Gifts to buy
- Things to make
- KaleidoSoul projects
- S.O.S. Cancer Journeys projects
- Things that need to be shipped
- Sugar-free cookies to bake
- Future work projects
- Art table ideas

It seems that the list making has gotten a little out of control!

I can always feel when Gabriella is on a rampage, because I start getting tension headaches and feel a distinctive tightening in my neck and shoulders. There is a specific anxiety that pervades my aura whenever I let Gabriella take the reins, and I know it's not healthy for me. Whenever I feel these warning signals in my body, I am reminded to take a step back.

Last week when I did this, I gave myself permission to not even *look* at my To-Do lists for a whole day. In that 24-hour respite, I was finally able to relax enough to sit in my comfy chair and "journey inside" in the silence. Gabriella was still chattering away about everything that needed to be done but I was able to explain that I needed a day off from The Lists. I politely thanked her for her skills and talents, then asked her to step back.

In the space of that inner stillness, a few of my other Neters were better able to come forward and share some wisdom with me. Julianna, my Inner Child, reminded me about the joy and magic of this holiday season. Mother Joy, my loving Inner Mother, shared with me the idea of making a To-Be list. "A To-Be list?" I exclaimed in puzzlement. "What on earth is that?"

She replied with her calm and tender wisdom. "Make a list of things you can do that help you simply *To Be*. What is it that brings you back to the present moment? What gives you a sense of balance, of being grounded?"

I thanked her for her wisdom and began creating a To-Be List which has zero potential to create tension headaches and tight shoulders! Here is part of my list:

- Sit in silence for 10 minutes
- Choose two SoulCollage® cards and journal with them
- Write a short prayer
- Watch a good TV show and do *absolutely nothing else* while watching
- Sip a cup of herbal tea and read a novel
- Take a walk by the ocean

During this rush-rush month of holiday preparations, perhaps you can give *yourself* some time off from your own To-Do lists. Let go of that age-old struggle of Do-Be Do-Be Do-Be Do.

Instead, let the end of that struggle be the BE instead of the DO.

Time for Reflection

Your challenge, should you decide to accept it, is to put everything down and simply watch the nine-minute guided imagery journey, *Guided*

Meditation for Holiday Stress Relief (see link below) by Glenda Cedarleaf, SoulCollage® Facilitator in North Carolina. Allow the short video to help you bring your soul back to balance. Do not (I repeat, do *not*) do anything else while you are watching. Allow yourself this little respite of peace.

After watching it, make your own To-Be List and post it where you'll see it every day.

Resource:

Guided Imagery Journey, *Guided Meditation for Holiday Stress Relief,* by SoulCollage® Facilitator Glenda Cedarleaf:
havenofrelaxation.com/holidaystressrelief

CHAPTER 50

ReGifting: ReVisited

OKAY, LET'S ALL just admit it right now. ReGifting is something we all do. I've done it, and you probably have too. A box of tempting chocolates just when you're cutting down on sugar. Ugly candles, potholders, certain books or CDs that just aren't "us." We receive something we don't like or want, and we put it in the closet (or the cupboard or the attic). Then it's holiday time and we need a gift for someone but don't know what to give them. Voila! We have an entire shelf of goodies to choose from.

I didn't grow up with the ReGifting process. I've only come to find its value as an adult. The first time I tried it, I was nervous and worried that someone would discover what I'd done. A well-meaning friend had given me a stone statue of several cats standing in a circle for my birthday. She knew I liked cats and I suppose she figured anything to do with cats would make me happy. Wrong!

Several months later, I carefully wrapped it back up and set it under the tree at our annual office party Yankee Swap. If you've never attended one of these, it's a fun game that involves choosing gifts and then actually taking gifts away from other people. To my happy surprise, one of my coworkers "stole" the cat statue from another person because he loved it so much.

I'm more comfortable now with the idea of ReGifting (as long as I don't mistakenly give it back to the person who gave it to me!). I also want to suggest yet another way to look at this, especially during the holidays when giving and gifts are on everyone's minds.

What if we practice ReGifting with some of the *inner* gifts that others give to us?

For instance, I receive generosity and affection in abundance from my husband Jeff. I could pass that gift of generosity on to everyone who crosses my path. My friend David gifts me with a genuine passion and childlike excitement for Christmas. I can absorb that enthusiasm and then regift it to the clerk in the corner drugstore who looks like she's having a bad day. My brother John gifts me with a listening ear when I need to talk about a problem that's weighing heavy on my mind. I can accept his gift and at the same time pass it on the next time a friend comes to me with a heavy heart and a story to share.

ReGifting doesn't always have to be about presents that we don't like. It can simply mean being aware of the gifts others give us (the unwrapped kind) and then consciously passing them on to others who also have need of them.

Time for Reflection

Make a list of some of your family members, friends, and pets along with the inner gifts that each one gives to you.

This week as you go about your daily busy-ness, make a conscious effort to pass on at least one of these gifts to someone who crosses your path.

Make a note of how this affects the creation of your SoulCollage® Community suit cards.

CHAPTER 51

Be Your Own Valentine

VALENTINE'S DAY IS coming soon, and the media is at it again. If you pay attention to all of the advertisements, it might seem like you're not really special unless your significant other surprises you with diamonds, a romantic dinner, and two dozen red roses.

My husband's idea of romance has nothing whatsoever to do with Valentine's Day. In fact, he somewhat "rebels" against all the media hype and would rather this particular "holiday" didn't exist. His own philosophy is that you should show people you love them every day of the year, not just on February 14.

Does this make me less special? I think not.

Then of course, there's the issue of whether or not you actually have a "significant other" to celebrate with. I didn't meet my husband until I was 35, so I've spent many a Valentine's Day alone.

Did spending all those Valentine's Days alone make me less special? Of course not.

My proposal to you, dear reader, is to kick up your energy just a little bit, and make a special effort of some kind to be *your own* special Valentine the next time February 14 rolls around. Make yourself a collage Valentine, address it to yourself and put it in the nearest mailbox tomorrow. Cook yourself a special dinner. Write yourself a love letter. Take yourself out to lunch. Send yourself flowers. Buy a box of your favorite chocolates and savor one thoroughly each day.

Even if you're in a loving relationship with a significant other, you can still take a few minutes on Valentine's Day to do something special for yourself. In the long run, the most precious relationship in your life is the one you have with yourself. Take some time this week to honor that.

Time for Reflection

Choose a pet name for yourself. You might use Sweetie Pie, Lambchops, Honey, Darling, Dah-ling, Baby . . . whatever name makes you smile inside. Mine is "Dear One."

Use this pet name whenever you need to step in and say something kind to yourself. Use it on your handmade Valentine to yourself. Tattoo it on your ankle. SoulCollage® it, or paint it in your journal.

Remember who you are: precious, loved, whole.

Everything I Need to Know About Life I Learned from Television

Overview

I was born in 1956 and have been watching television all my life. I grew up on the *Ed Sullivan Show*, *The Brady Bunch*, and *My Three Sons*. As a teen, I bonded with my dad over dramas such as *Marcus Welby, M.D.* and *Hawaii Five-O*. Later in my life I found myself drawn to sitcoms that made me laugh as well as dramas about family life and relationships.

For many years I felt guilty about my infatuation with television. The guilt lifted once I realized that the reason I am drawn to certain shows is that they are telling important stories. As I began the practice of SoulCollage®, I discovered more of my inner parts and archetypal influences by paying careful attention to the characters in my favorite shows.

The essays included here speak to the power of story to inform our lives in ways that invite insight and transformation. *Grey's Anatomy*, *Judging Amy*, *The Middle*, *The Big C*, *Gilmore Girls*, *Ally McBeal*, *Without a Trace*, and a couple of reality shows all make an appearance in this section. I hope that the inner awareness I received from these stories will enlighten you as well as inspire you to look for the influential power of story whenever you turn on your television, watch a movie, or read a novel.

CHAPTER 52

Good Mothering

WHEN I WAS laid up in bed several years ago with bronchitis, I started watching *Judging Amy* reruns every day and immediately got hooked. If you're not familiar with this show, it's about a Juvenile Court judge (Amy) who is in her thirties and lives at home with her mother (Maxine), a social worker. Amy has a 10-year-old daughter named Lauren. While I found the courtroom scenes, the social work stories, and the love triangles intriguing, I still wasn't quite sure why I was so drawn to this show.

A few of my inner voices were intent on judging me for this prime time obsession. *Can't you find something better to do with your time? This is ridiculous. You're becoming a TV junkie!*

In spite of this, somewhere deep within me I felt the need to keep watching. It felt like something more than just a television show, so I decided to trust the other inner voices who were nudging me to continue watching. I chose to trust my intuition, and developed a "wait and see" attitude as I continued to watch episode after episode, season after season.

While all of this was happening, I did a SoulCollage® reading where I asked a question of my deck, and then drew four random cards. Interestingly enough, three of those four cards had something to do with the topic of *mothering*.

As I continued with this reading, I discovered something wonderful!

Here is part of what my Divine Mother card (see link below) said to me as part of this reading:

Good, truly deep mothering is not something that you ever received, although your mom's intentions were good. You are now struggling with the process of inner mothering. I can help you with this. Watching Judging Amy *is helping you too. Do not brush it aside as "just another TV show . . ." You are receiving much wisdom and insight from watching Maxine with Amy, and Amy with Lauren. Embrace what you are learning there. Be glad of it and grateful for it as well.*

I was completely startled to see those words flow from my heart to my hand to the paper! Everything became clear to me as soon as I wrote those words. Crystal clear. From then on, whenever I watched the show, I had a focus, and the lessons I learned about what it means to lovingly mother myself came faster than I could write them down.

As a result of these insights, I pulled my inner Good Mother card out from my deck and added an image of Amy and Maxine (see link below). Whenever this card appears in a reading, I am instantly reminded of the mothering lessons I learned from watching this drama so many years ago.

I love telling this story about myself because it's a clear reminder of how I should always trust my intuition. I've also learned not to judge myself for wherever my soul is leading me, even if it's guiding me to watch television! My soul truly does know what will serve me best. All I have to do is listen and follow.

Time for Reflection

Do you have a SoulCollage® card for the part of you who trusts your deepest intuition? If not, be on the lookout for images that speak this truth to you.

Take a look at the television shows you are inexplicably drawn to. Is there one that brings you pleasure but you resist watching? Try, for one day, to set aside the critical inner voices that might be telling you to stop watching it.

Notice what inner voices are urging you to watch this show. Trust these voices. Give yourself permission to watch it as much as you like.

Be open as the weeks and months go by for the lessons that are winging their way to you on the stories that the show is telling.

SoulCollage® Example

Please visit KaleidoSoul.com/into-the-heart-tv
The password for this page is: story

The topic to scroll down to is:
Judging Amy

CHAPTER 53

I See You

THERE IS A scene from *Judging Amy* that went straight from the screen and into my heart, where it will stay always, because it illustrated the kind of compassion we are to have with all our inner voices. For months, my therapist had been trying to get me to be kind and nonjudgmental whenever a particularly shadowy voice would rise up inside me. I found this a difficult concept to grasp, until I saw this particular episode. Then, everything shifted into focus.

In the scene, Amy is in the courtroom listening to the case of a young teenager who is in trouble with the law. As she tries to question him, he alternates between hiding his head in his shirt and hollering expletives at her. He shouts that she might as well send him away because no one ever hears him or sees him, and he knows that this is what happens to "kids like him."

It soon becomes apparent that the boy's mother has left his family; he is wildly angry and grieving this unexpected loss. Finally, Amy faces the boy, who has hidden his head underneath his jacket. She stops asking questions and simply sits with him in compassionate silence.

After a while, in the presence of this patient woman, the boy tentatively stops hiding, making eye contact with her for the first time. "I see you . . ." she says, and in her voice is the exact kindness and compassion that my therapist was telling me about. "I *see* you . . ."

Whenever I'm faced with one of my own more difficult inner voices, I remember this scene from *Judging Amy*. I remember Amy's still posture, the kind look in her eyes, and the loving sound of her voice. And then, I am also able to say, "I hear you . . . I see you" to the shadowy parts of myself.

Time for Reflection

The next time you are confronted by one of your shadowed inner parts, make it a point to sit still with this part of you and patiently listen to its whole story. See if you can get to the place where you can sit with this inner voice and hold the intention of *not* sending it away. See if you can say, "I see you . . ." with compassion and non-judgment to this often misunderstood part of your being.

Think of your favorite television shows. Which ones stimulate your imagination as well as entertain you? Choose a favorite character on television and conduct an imaginary conversation with him or her. You can do this in your imagination, or write it out in your journal. What can you learn from this character? What gifts do they bring you?

CHAPTER 54

Pick Me, Choose Me, Love Me

I WASN'T ALWAYS a *Grey's Anatomy* fan. A friend told me about it during the second season; I watched one episode and was hooked! Then I rented the entire first season and watched every episode, one right after the other. I loved the show for its characters, its rich stories about relationships, survivors, love, living, and dying.

But there was one episode that caught me so deep inside, it brought me up short and made me wonder what had hit me. It's the show where Derek (aka "McDreamy") is confronted by Meredith (the intern he's falling in love with) because his ex-wife has come back into his life. She is hurt because he is considering "doing the right thing" and going back to his ex-wife even though he doesn't love her. Meredith gives Derek a passionate speech about how much she loves him, and then begs him to choose between her and his ex. "Pick *me*. Choose *me*. Love *me*."

She delivered these words with such conviction that I found myself on the edge of my seat, hugging the couch pillow to my stomach, doubled over, and weeping. Not just a tear trickling down, but gut-wrenching cries. It felt like someone had kicked me in the stomach.

The episode ended and I cried a little more, went to bed, slept, woke up, and went on with my days. But that whole incident was embedded in my mind, my heart, my soul. After several days of mulling it over in the back of my mind, I realized that my intense emotional reaction had to do with a whole lot more than a television show about doctors, interns and love affairs.

I realized this because the scene kept re-playing itself in my mind. Over and over and over. The feelings that those six words (Pick *me*.

Choose *me*. Love *me*.) evoked in me ran a whole lot deeper than an ordinary television show scenario would suggest.

I remained curious about my response to that seemingly innocuous scene. I sensed some wisdom inherent there, something for me to learn about myself. So I didn't berate myself for reacting so viscerally and emotionally to a TV drama. I just let it be.

And then one day, it came to me. I can't tell you exactly what triggered this knowing (although I'm sure my openness had plenty to do with it), but a few weeks later my exaggerated response suddenly made sense.

As you may already know, a big part of my identity is that of "stepmother." My husband Jeff has three children from his first marriage and I helped raise the two older ones, Amanda and Jeffrey. Their mother made all of our lives very difficult for most of those growing-up years. It took a fictional character in a TV drama to help me admit that this was a huge source of my own pain and sorrow during the kids' adolescence. *I had secretly hoped, all along, that they would pick **me**, choose **me**, instead of their mother.* But every time, no matter how she treated them, they always chose her.

This was a huge learning for me. I was able to see that my own unrealistic (although certainly understandable) expectations were the cause of so much sadness and struggle for me as I tried to help Jeff bring Amanda and Jeffrey into a sane and loving adulthood. And I was able to accept for the first time how and why the kids chose their mother every time.

I was finally able to embrace that part of me who only wanted to love Jeff's children and to be loved in return. I was finally able to *hear* the wounded voice inside me who wasn't the "chosen" one. I even created a SoulCollage® card to express this part of me (see link below).

I am still totally amazed at (and grateful for) those six simple words from a fictional television character, because they allowed one of my own locked-away inner voices to see the light of day again.

Time for Reflection

Are there any parts of your personal history that still hold sorrow and pain for you? If so, journal about how unrealistic expectations (however reasonable at the time) may have had an effect on that distress. Create a card about that time in your life and allow it to speak to you and tell you its story.

The next time you seemingly "overreact" to something (a song on the radio, a line spoken on TV, a paragraph in a novel), don't judge yourself. Simply watch and wait and be with the feelings, be with whatever your reaction is bringing up for you. Allow it to just be there in your heart. Trust that eventually, if you give it room to breathe, its lesson will be clearer to you.

SoulCollage® Example

Please visit KaleidoSoul.com/into-the-heart-tv
The password for this page is: story

The topic to scroll down to is:
Pick Me. Choose Me.

CHAPTER 55

Luke's Dark Day

FOR ME, GILMORE *Girls* is like reading a never-ending, intelligent, quirky, amazing novel without having to expend the energy of picking up a book! I watched all seven seasons in 2011 during my "chemo days" and then once again last summer just for the joy of it.

One episode in particular (Season 5, Episode 10) really spoke to my soul.

One of the characters in this series is Luke Danes. He is a 30-something confirmed bachelor who is sometimes grumpy, but an integral part of the small Connecticut community where the show takes place. In this particular episode, there is a celebration going on for Miss Patti, the town's colorful dance teacher. She is celebrating 40 years of being in "show biz."

At the same time, Luke is having a difficult celebration of his own. On the 30th of every November, he simply disappears. No one knows where he goes or what he does on this particular day every year. The community doesn't question it, and they certainly don't ask him about it.

Enter Lorelai Gilmore, a single mother also in her thirties. She and Luke have begun a relationship, and she is curious about his disappearing act. When she questions him about where he goes on the 30th of November, he says, "I disappear. I don't work. I don't talk to anyone. I get in a funk. I have a dark day. I don't like to talk about it."

It turns out that his dad died on the 30th of November over a decade ago and this is Luke's way of dealing with his feelings about that loss. He gives himself a day to feel the anger and the sadness surrounding his deep grief. Just that *one* day, as he called it, a "dark day." Then he returns and goes back to his life as usual.

"What an excellent idea!" I thought as the episode unfolded. When sorrowful feelings come, why *not* give ourselves a day to feel those feelings, embrace them, and let them be? I could give myself a "Dark Day" every year on the 15th of July in honor of the day that my beloved cat Sasha died. Or on the 4th of March to grieve my mother. I could choose a random day every year to let myself feel the sadness about my decision not to have children in this lifetime.

I loved this insight. But there was more.

When the 30th of November came, Luke didn't leave town right away. In the morning, he went to visit Lorelai for a few minutes and she got him to open up about his father just the tiniest bit. He had put his dad's unfinished boat in storage and refused to look at it for 15 years, but on this "Dark Day" he was forced to look at it because the storage place was closing down and he had to move it. Lorelai helps him out by storing the boat for him in her own small garage.

He connects with Lorelai three times on this "Dark Day," and this is a huge step for him, to be with another person on a day when he usually doesn't see or talk to anyone. Towards the end of this episode, he is actually attending Miss Patti's Celebration, and while he isn't exactly bubbling over with joy and enthusiasm, he has the softened look of someone who thought he was alone and suddenly realizes he is part of a community.

There is much wisdom here for all of us. If you need a "Dark Day," go ahead and give that to yourself. Wrap your grief around you like a soft velvet blanket and give yourself to it for 24 hours. If you need to reach out to someone and share your anguish, give that to yourself instead. There is a time and a place for both . . . and each can be equally healing. It's all a matter of what *you* need at any particular time.

Time for Reflection

Have you ever allowed yourself a "Dark Day?" If so, describe it in your journal. If not, describe what your own "Dark Day" would be like.

Make a SoulCollage® card that expresses your "Dark Day" (real or imagined).

Make a list of people in your life with whom it would be safe to share the details of your "Dark Day."

The next time you find that you are holding on to grief or anger, set the intention to share it with a trusted friend or family member, either in writing or in person.

Make a SoulCollage® card to represent the absolute fact that you are not alone in this world.

CHAPTER 56

Time Release SoulCollage®

IN ONE OF my favorite episodes of the sitcom *The Middle*, 14-year-old Sue is worried that her brother Brick is not "getting" the true meaning of Christmas. Brick has been spending hours talking with the young minister at their church. Reverend Tim Tom (no, that's not a misprint!) has been answering all of Brick's questions, but Sue notices that her brother is still full of doubt.

At one point, Sue turns to Reverend Tim Tom and says, "You're not going to give up on him, right? You're going to write him some special soul-saving song, aren't you?" Then she pauses, trying to keep up with the thoughts that are going through her young mind. Something important occurs to her and she looks at him in wonder as she slowly says, "Or is this one of those time release things where everything you've said will kick in later?"

I laughed out loud at this. The incongruity of comparing a time-release cold medicine capsule to a major spiritual truth filled me with delight, mainly because I know firsthand the feeling of "time release wisdom." Twenty years ago my spiritual director answered a red-hot question I had about where my father "went" after he had died. I was grieving greatly, and his answer made no sense to me at the time. This is what he said to me: *I don't know where he is exactly, but I do know that wherever he is, he is closer to you now than he ever was when he was here in his body.* I remember his answer almost word for word, and even though I didn't understand it at the time, I had the feeling deep in my bones that his answer was correct.

His answer is much clearer to me now. Thanks to the effect of "time release wisdom," I have much more experience and emotional maturity supporting me now. I've also survived the deaths of my mother, a few close friends, and three dearly beloved felines. My spiritual director's answer made a little more sense each time I experienced another deep loss, and now it makes complete sense to me.

This "time release" thing is very true of our SoulCollage® practice as well. I might make a card today, find it totally baffling, and place it in my deck where it rests, seemingly forgotten. Several months from now when it surfaces again, its message is easier to understand. I can pose a question to my deck and receive clear, consistent answers to my question from the cards I draw in my reading, but next week a friend might reference a movie character or a story she's just read, and I will add this information to what the cards already told me in my reading.

This is exactly how the process of SoulCollage® "works." The wisdom of each card we make works within our deepest being. As time passes, our cards continue to release in us their individual and specific wisdom. What a way to grow!

Time for Reflection

Take a look through your deck and make note of any "Mystery" cards you have. These are cards that haven't been forthcoming as to their meaning. Just notice these cards. Smile gently, bow to them, thank the images for merging into your life, and then place them reverently back in your deck.

Bide your time, be patient with yourself, and know that in time, the messages will be clearer, the wisdom released.

CHAPTER 57

The Bitch Is Back

AFTER STRUGGLING WITH the concept of Bitch as an archetypal energy for years, it all came clear to me recently during episode six of the second season of *The Big C*. The main character, Cathy Jamison, is a 40-something high school teacher who has been diagnosed with Stage 4 melanoma. At this point in the story, she has had a successful round of treatments and is beginning a new clinical trial. The Girl's Swim Team coach has left for greener pastures, so Cathy steps up and volunteers. She was a medal-winning swimmer in high school and college. She loves to swim and is choosing to coach because it makes her happy and she is good at it.

After a few practices, the parents begin to protest. They gather together with the principal to try to oust her from the coaching position. They say many hurtful things to her out of their own ignorance. *The fact is you have cancer. Who knows what else will go wrong for you this year? How can you do this if you are in and out of hospitals? Everyone's afraid to say no to the lady with cancer.*

Cathy steps right up to the group and forcefully says, "I'd tell you to take your pity and shove it, but I don't care. You might have hired me for the wrong reasons but if you want to fire the 'lady with cancer,' you'd better hire a damned good lawyer."

Then one of the female parents says, under her breath, "What a bitch!"

Cathy replies, "Yeah, I am a bitch. I'm a tough, brave bitch and if you let me, I will turn all these girls into tough, brave bitches too. We can go all the way to the championship. Now if you don't mind, I'm going to take my team, whoever's still on it, for a run." She leaves the pool area, walking tall and strong as the positive, balanced energy of Bitch shines from her.

As soon as I saw that scene, I hit the reverse button on our DVR and watched it a few more times. "So that's what balanced archetypal Bitch energy looks like," I thought, grinning to myself in delight. I finally could see that being in tune with balanced Bitch energy is a very positive and powerful thing. If we have too much of that energy, we become crazed and out of control. If we don't have enough of it, we become doormats, not owning our own power, letting people walk all over us.

Someone on our KaleidoSoul SoulCollage® Yahoo Group recently wrote that BITCH stands for *Babe in Total Control of Herself.* I loved hearing that but I didn't really understand it, probably because I didn't have a lot of role models for balanced Bitch energy when I was growing up.

I was so moved by finally "getting" this archetypal energy that I made a SoulCollage® card for my own Council Bitch (see link below). There are three women on it and I realize now that one is young, one is middle-aged, and one is older, so for me it's a good representation of the totality of a woman's life. This card captures the power and positive strength of Bitch energy in balance. This Neter says to me:

We Are the Ones Who are strong and balanced and centered and stable and holding our ground. We Are the Ones Who know who we are. We Are the Ones Who protect the borderlines of your personal boundaries. We Are the Ones Who don't take crap from anyone, including those in your inner world. We Are the Ones Who protect you, who enable you to keep yourself safe. We Are the Ones Who have erect yet relaxed posture. We Are the Ones Who are fierce and determined to keep you safe. We may be called Bitch by others in a negative way but we know that this is a positive label and we enjoy it! We Are the Ones Who stand tall and proud and determined. We Are the Ones Who clearly know who we are so we can create and hold and keep these boundaries safe.

Our gift to you is the strength and purpose and focus to remember Who You Are at all times!

Time for Reflection

Take some time this week to sit with the idea of *balanced* Bitch energy. See if you can find any examples in literature, movies, songs, or television.

Gather some images and make your own Bitch card, either for the archetypal energy (Council Suit), or for an inner voice (Committee Suit) who has its bitch-ness in balance.

What happens when there is too much Bitch energy in your life? What happens when there is not enough Bitch energy in your life?

SoulCollage® Example

Please visit KaleidoSoul.com/into-the-heart-tv
The password for this page is: story

The topic to scroll down to is:
Bitch

CHAPTER 58

Imperfectly Beautiful

SEVERAL YEARS AGO there was an amazing television show that was popular here in America. It was called *How to Look Good Naked*. The host was Carson Kressley, a quirky and compassionate man whose main quest was to change women's perceptions about their bodies.

In the first show, he was working with a 32-year-old woman named Layla, who was 30 pounds overweight and struggling with self-esteem. She put on a bathing suit and then stood with Carson in front of several full-length mirrors. He asked her to tell him what she saw. Predictably enough, she talked about the flaws: her arms were flabby; she hated her thighs; her legs were too short. Can you relate?

Then Carson told her what *he* saw. He described her beautiful skin, her luscious cleavage, how her curves were in just the right places.

He stood behind her with his hands on her shoulders and invited her to see herself the way he saw her. "Here's Layla," he said, looking into the mirror with her. "Is she perfect? No. Is she beautiful? Yes."

It was a lesson not only for Layla, but for the millions of women watching.

Repeat after me: *Am I perfect? Certainly not! Am I beautiful anyway, in spite of my imperfections? Certainly yes!*

Time for Reflection

Stand in front of a full-length mirror and make note of what you see. If you're like Layla, you'll probably list your imperfections first. That's okay.

Then pause. Invite your own version of Carson Kressley to stand beside you at the mirror. This can be either a real person or an imaginary one. It doesn't matter, as long as it is someone who looks at you nonjudgmentally and with genuine kindness.

Allow this being to describe the beautiful parts of you that he/she sees.

Affirm to yourself (many times throughout your days) *I don't have to be perfect to be beautiful.*

Make a SoulCollage® card for the Imperfectly Beautiful You.

CHAPTER 59

So You Think You Can SoulCollage®

MY HUSBAND AND I love *So You Think You Can Dance,* which is a competitive reality show. The top 20 dancers are randomly assigned partners, choreographers, and dance styles. They then compete for the judges' praise and the audience's votes. Eventually it all comes down to one person winning the title "America's Favorite Dancer."

It's competitive in the sense that there is one winner. But there's another kind of competition going on, I've noticed, and that is a contest of the inner kind. The dancers are expected to learn dance styles that are different from their training, so it very quickly becomes a matter of pushing one's own boundaries. For example, this season a classically trained ballerina found herself doing Hip Hop, Jazz, and Latin Ballroom. A street dancer without any training at all found himself doing the Tango, the Paso Doble, and Bollywood.

I am always amazed at the versatility of these young dancers, and am thrilled beyond belief when one of them pushes their own boundaries and "nails" a dance performance that a week ago they never would have considered doing.

Which brings me to SoulCollage®. You knew I was getting here sooner or later, didn't you? I think it's important that once in a while, in our personal practice of this wonderful process, we push our own boundaries a little bit. Just a little, that's all it takes. For example, I noticed that I've been resisting facilitating a workshop on the Transpersonal Cards because I didn't think I understood them well enough. Which is a little silly, since I already have all three cards in my deck. So I reached beyond my comfort zone and offered a workshop on this topic. Guess what? With a little research, practice, and some positive inner self-talk, I think it went pretty well!

Time for Reflection

Do something SoulCollagey this month that pushes your own inner boundaries a little bit. Here are some ideas:

Is there a card you've been meaning to create but keep putting off for some reason or other? Challenge yourself to make that card this month.

If you're a Kindred Spirit Member (see link below), listen to one of the 100+ SoulCollage® recordings in our Members Only Audio Library and see what it inspires in you.

Print out a few back issues of our free KaleidoSoul monthly newsletter, *Soul Songs,* on topics that pique your interest (see link below).

Read one of Seena Frost's articles on her website (see link below) and notice what interests you the most.

Sit down and journal with a card you made a long time ago that maybe scares you just a little bit.

Be brave. You can trust this process.

SoulCollage® Resources

Visit this page for more information about KaleidoSoul Kindred Spirits:
kaleidosoul.com/members

Visit this page to see back issues of our free monthly newsletter, *Soul Songs*, categorized by topics:
kaleidosoul.com/soulsongsbackissues

Visit this page for some of Seena Frost's articles about SoulCollage®:
soulcollage.com/seena-frost/articles-by-seena-frost

CHAPTER 60

Dancing Babies and Long-Gone Aunts

THERE'S A WONDERFUL scene in an old *Ally McBeal* television episode that I love to refer to when talking about the SoulCollage® Committee Suit. If you've never seen it, *Ally McBeal* was a delightful comedy about a quirky lawyer living in Boston in the 1990's.

In this scene, Ally is telling John Cage (another lawyer, even more idiosyncratic than Ally) about how a small dancing baby has been following her around. This baby has been appearing to her at the strangest moments and it's starting to drive her crazy. She has tried ignoring this imaginary baby, and she has even tried kick-boxing it out of her life, but it still continues to "haunt" her.

At this point, John tells her about a time in his own life when he kept dreaming about his long-deceased aunt, who kept insisting that he have tea with her.

Ally is fascinated, because John's problem sounds so similar to her own. "So what did you do to stop the annoying dreams about your aunt?" she asks.

"Simple," John replies. "I had tea with her."

I think of this in relation to all of my own parts that make up my inner Committee. If there's one that's really pestering me for attention, then the very best thing for me to do is to sit down with it and listen. Instead of ignoring it, or trying to kick it away in frustration, I invite it into my inner playroom and have a tea party with it.

Time for Reflection

Are there any dancing babies and/or long-deceased relatives following *you* around this week? Are there other inner voices that are acting out and causing you bewildering moments of embarrassment? Write about them in your journal.

Instead of wishing they would go away, simply name them and find time to sit down with them. You can do this by making SoulCollage® cards for them or by asking them "Who are you?" and journaling their answers for several minutes.

CHAPTER 61

Lost and Found

SEVERAL YEARS AGO I found myself captivated by *Without a Trace*. I love a good drama but I'm not usually drawn to programs that focus on crime and violence. This one delves into both, so I was puzzled when I found myself eagerly watching it week after week. At first I was just keeping my husband company because he really liked the show, but after a while I realized that I was completely fascinated with the main characters (Jack, Martin, and Samantha) who work for the Missing Persons Unit of the New York City FBI.

Each week they searched for a different person who had gone missing "without a trace." Children, teens, adults, seniors. Handicapped. Dark-skinned. Pale. There was even one in a wedding gown! It was amazing to watch these brilliant minds as they sought clues and, in most cases, found those who were lost.

I was just beginning my practice with SoulCollage® when I was drawn into this show, and after a couple of seasons of incredibly powerful storylines, I finally recognized the metaphor. Various people were missing; this FBI team worked diligently to find them. In my own life, various parts of *me* were missing, and I was just coming to realize that I could be the one to sleuth them out of hiding!

Jung talks about these parts of ourselves who have disappeared as the "golden shadow." They are the bright and shining parts of us who have been lost or buried along the way. For me, some of these parts included: the fiction writer, the artist, and the joyful inner child. As I continued to watch *Without a Trace*, I was able to *remember* each of these inner parts. Then I was able to recall how much they meant to me, how once upon a time they were each a vital part of my life. Finally, I was able to search in my inner sanctuary for them, apologize for burying them in the shadows, and bring them back into my daily life.

Just as in the procedural episodes, it was not a simple task! But it was a joyful one. In the final scenes of the TV show there is usually a reunion of some sort. People who have lost a loved one rejoiced over the fact that they were found. And so I rejoice today. I have found a way to integrate my fiction writer, my artist, and my inner child into my daily life. They are no longer "lost." I have finally "found" parts of myself who are integral to my being.

Time for Reflection

Are there parts of you who have "gone missing?" Parts that used to be important to you? Ponder this question for a week or so. Jot down any ideas that come to you. Trust your intuition.

Make a SoulCollage® card for one of these "lost" inner parts. Journal with it. Ask it to tell you its story. Get in touch with its energy again. Remember why it was so important to you. Apologize to this *lost and found* part for ignoring it for so long. Allow yourself to receive its forgiveness.

Find a way to integrate this part into your daily life.

Rejoice that a part of you that was lost is now found!

Difficult Times

Overview

No matter where we live, what we believe, or what our work in the world is, one thing that every human being has in common is that difficult times are a part of our life journeys. There is no avoiding these "unexpected journeys." They are a part of life.

SoulCollage® can help us through life's many difficulties by helping us embrace whatever it is that we are going through. Making cards about the fear, sadness, or anger invoked by a challenging situation can offer release and a different way of viewing it. Doing a reading to ask for guidance and support can offer surprising suggestions and solutions that we wouldn't have thought of on our own.

The Stoic philosopher Epictetus once said, "It's not what happens to you, but how you react to it that matters." The stories in this section express how SoulCollage® empowered me to transform my reactions to difficult times, such as a cancer diagnosis, my husband's legal blindness, and the terrorist attacks of September 11, 2001. I hope that you will also find ways to use SoulCollage® to empower your own unexpected journeys.

CHAPTER 62

Healing Our Wounds – Remembering 9/11

FIVE HOURS IN the emergency room one beautiful summer afternoon. A box of bandaids. Ten antibiotic pills. Half a tube of Bacitracin. This list tells the story of an infected fingernail that took three weeks to finally begin to heal.

One tiny little hangnail is how it began. But the journey to healing this little nuisance wasn't as simple as I expected. Three weeks is a looooong time when you're waiting for an infection to go away. I discovered that many of my "inner voices" were highly activated because of this one tiny little infection.

For example:

Inner Critic (Ethel): How could you have been so stupid as to bite that nail down so far before going for your manicure?

Worrywart: I just know this is going to turn into blood poisoning, and then we will die.

Impatience: It's not healing fast enough.

Worrywart: It's going to get infected again.

Judge: What on earth is wrong with that stupid doctor? I don't think he really got all of the infection out.

Inner Critic: I knew you should have asked for a different doctor.

Scared Inner Child: Hey, this hurts a lot. I want some love and attention.

Inner Mother: Sweetie, you can skip washing the dishes until it's all healed. I'll run a warm bath for you. Would you like that?

Well, you get the idea. As the days went by and healing still wasn't visible, parts of me got panicky and anxious and downright cranky.

What I forgot during the weeks that my finger was healing is that our wounds and injuries often heal when we're not looking. It's a very simple truth, but one that I often overlook when faced with a stressful situation like this one.

Looking back on my life, I remember times when the hurt was so deep I thought I would never heal. The broken leg. The lover who left me. The stepchild who rejected me. The death of my father. The cancer diagnosis. The loss of a beloved cat.

Yet, when I think of these wounds today, I feel no bitter pain; I sense no anguish. I am simply awed by the wonder of how time and space really do heal our bodies, minds, and spirits.

On September 11, 2001, America was wounded deeply when the Twin Towers in New York City were attacked. This is a wound that is much more severe and unfathomable than a broken leg or an infected finger. Yet deep as that wound was, it too is a wound that is healing. Very, *very* slowly, in the tiniest of increments, our country's worst wound *is* healing.

The important thing is to trust the process of healing, to remember that if it takes a tiny little fingernail infection three weeks to heal, then how much longer it might take to heal a broken heart, a lost relationship, a shattered bone. It's even more important to give your own wounds time and space to heal. Ask for help from doctors, therapists, friends, family, animals, and of course, Spirit.

Time for Reflection

Look back today and remember September 11, 2001. Where were you when you heard the news? How did you feel? Which of your inner parts reacted to that tragedy?

If you were not in America at that time, remember a tragic event that injured your own country. Where were you when you heard the news? How did you feel? What inner parts of you reacted to that tragedy?

Pay attention to those inner parts that were hurt, scared, angry, or terrified. Acknowledge them. Listen to them.

Do they still have things to say about that day? Write out a dialog, like mine above.

Make SoulCollage® cards for one or more of these parts.

Can you notice any healing that has taken place in these parts since then or are they still bearing the wound?

Make a list of wounds (physical, emotional, spiritual) you have received throughout your life. Have any of them healed? Are there some that still need your time and love and attention?

CHAPTER 63

Bright Side of the Road

My barn having burned down,
I can now see the moon.

~ ZEN KOAN

IT HAS BEEN many years but I still recall the exact scenario at the moment I was diagnosed with breast cancer. I remember exactly where I was (at work), what time it was (5:45 p.m.), and who I was with (my kind coworker, John, sitting to my left). I remember the exact words the doctor said as I sat stunned, holding the receiver in my left hand. "There are some cancerous cells in your left breast."

Talk about a barn burning down! Nine words from a doctor, and my whole life came to a screeching halt. The next seven months were occupied with surgeries, chemo treatments, wig shopping, support group meetings, radiation sessions, and lots of long naps.

I hadn't heard of SoulCollage® when my "barn burned down." Even though it was almost three years after my treatments were over before I participated in my first SoulCollage® workshop, my heart was still longing for healing. SoulCollage® was the full "moon" that shone its light on my trauma, my fear, my anger, and then finally . . . my own inner radiance.

Soon after I learned about SoulCollage®, I created several cards around the theme of my breast cancer experience (see link below). Simply recognizing these Neters through the process of SoulCollage®

brought a fine, clean healing to my wounded body and soul. Giving image to these voices only served to intensify the healing. Dialoging with them and then finally accepting them was a bright blessing beyond belief.

So yes, breast cancer was an insidious, unwelcome pyromaniac that wreaked havoc in my world. There were many days (even after the treatments were over) when I didn't want to get out of bed. Yes, cancer had definitely "burned down my barn."

But there's a bright side even to something like this. With the "barn" down, I could now see "the moon." For me, this moon showed itself in a variety of ways: my husband's rock-solid support and love, the gift of taking time off and eventually moving away from a job that was no longer serving me, a closer relationship with my oldest brother, a certain knowing that I was cherished by so many people, inspiration to write the book *Bright Side of the Road*, two new friends (also survivors) I had met online who held my hand and talked me through the whole seven months, and my dear wise-woman therapist Fran, who I would not have found if not for my diagnosis.

My point in sharing these thoughts with you is this: there is *nothing* that can happen to you that is too big for healing. Nothing. If something happens (or has already happened) to you that feels like the end of the world, know this: you can get through it. You *will* get through it. And SoulCollage® will be the moon that shines its luminous light on your pain and brokenness. The practice of SoulCollage® will be the glue that puts your world back together.

Time for Reflection

Think of a time in your life when your own "barn" burned down. Perhaps it's happening right now in some way.

Begin to use SoulCollage® to work your way through it. Listen to the voices inside of you who have something to say about what happened (or is happening). Let them have their say. Honor them with SoulCollage® cards.

Make a card or cards to give image to some archetypal guides who can offer you comfort and strength. For example: Healer, Mother, Wise One.

Create an "I am a survivor" Committee card to remind you of your own inner strength. Allow the healing to happen.

SoulCollage® Examples

Please visit KaleidoSoul.com/breastcancer
and
KaleidoSoul.com/cancer-journey

CHAPTER 64

Things Happen

Every time I think that I'm getting old, and gradually
going to the grave,
something else happens.

~ ELVIS PRESLEY

I REMEMBER A week several years ago when everything was going smoothly for me. I thought my life was perfectly on track. I had left my job at our local nonprofit theatre, having been there way too long and feeling like I was being called in another direction. Yet the theatre was a home-away-from-home for me, so I decided to volunteer as an usher.

Then, just as I was smugly congratulating myself for solving the problem of how to let go without actually letting go, *something else happened!* A person I'd thought of as a close friend spread some lies about me to people at the theatre and I was notified that my services were no longer needed as a volunteer. Talk about shock! I was flooded with feelings of anger, betrayal, and loss.

In the wake of this inner chaos, I went to my SoulCollage® deck and tearfully pulled two cards out. As I randomly chose the cards, I asked the question, *"Who is going to help me with this situation? Who is going to help me get through this?"*

One of the cards I drew was my Peaceful Warrior who spoke to me of protecting my inner tribe, standing centered so as not to be thrown off balance, and settling arguments peacefully without violence.

The other card I drew was my Angel of Sorrow. This Neter told me there was grieving left undone from choosing to leave a job and people I'd known for ten years and had considered family. I journaled with these two cards and even propped them up by the phone for a shot of visual courage when I called my ex-boss at the theatre in order to speak the truth.

Yes, *things happen*. Confusing, hurtful things. Sad, grievous things. Shocking, horrible things. Usually when we least expect them to. It's a fact of life. Our job is not to rail against these things when they happen, but to somehow find the inner grace and courage to accept them. For me, SoulCollage® is a splendid path that helps me to accept and embrace everything that happens to me on my inner and outer journeys.

Time for Reflection

What has happened to you in the last several months? Name some things that you weren't expecting, good or bad.

Has something "happened" to you recently that you are still resisting? What would happen if you let go and invited it in?

Go to your SoulCollage® deck and choose two cards at random, then listen to what they have to say to you about your situation. If you don't have any cards yet, just choose a couple of images instead. Let their wisdom guide you.

SoulCollage® Example

Please visit KaleidoSoul.com/into-the-heart-hard-times
The password for this page is: journey

The topic to scroll down to is:
Things Happen

SoulCollage® Resource

Visit this page for more information about doing a random card reading:
kaleidosoul.com/cardreadings

CHAPTER 65

The Katrina Trees

AT FIRST GLANCE, the sculpture simply looks like a beautiful wooden carving of herons (see link below). After a closer look, we see that these birds were created from a dead oak tree in Biloxi, Mississippi, USA. The oak tree was one of hundreds of saltwater casualties that resulted from Hurricane Katrina, which ravaged the Biloxi coastline in 2005.

This sculpture is actually a wonderful tribute to the fact that when devastation occurs, possibilities still exist.

Biloxi's Katrina sculpture project began in 2007 when Mayor A.J. Holloway spoke with Mississippi "chainsaw artist" Dayton Scoggins about sculpting marine-related figures from the dozens of standing dead trees in the median of Beach Boulevard in Biloxi. After work crews "topped" the dead trees, Scoggins made the first of two sculpting visits to Biloxi, creating egrets, seagulls, pelicans, and dolphins from a collection of trees just west of the Biloxi Lighthouse.

Scoggins's initial five sculptures inspired Florida sculptor Marlin Miller to approach the city about donating his time and talent to sculpting more standing dead trees in the center medians in Biloxi. Miller, who exhibits sculptures at shows nationally, wanted to leave his mark on Biloxi and return the favor of Biloxians who had helped his community recover after Hurricane Ivan a couple of years earlier.

There are now 20 such amazing works of art in Biloxi, and you can see many of them in a short slideshow (see link below).

I first read about these Katrina Trees in the wonderful novel *The Beach Trees* by Karen White. I was moved to tears reading about them and how they came to be. Like you, I am no stranger to devastation.

The lesson that artists Scoggins and Miller give to us through these beautiful carvings is simply this: no matter what has happened to us in our lives, no matter what has "brought us down," beautiful possibilities still remain.

It is up to us, it is *always* up to us, to pick ourselves up after the hurricanes of our lives have abated. After rising from the wreckage, we are to seek for ways to create beauty from the damage.

In my own life, SoulCollage® is one way that I can create wholeness and brilliance from any devastating event that has affected my days. When I give image to my personal hurricanes and converse with them, they show me their beauty. They empower me to transform any "dead trees" in my own life into beautiful works of art for the entire world to see.

Time for Reflection

What personal "hurricanes" have you encountered and survived on your life's journey?

Choose one "personal hurricane" and give it a name. For example: Hurricane Cancer, Hurricane Divorce, Hurricane Bankruptcy . . . etc.

Journal about this Hurricane in your life. What was destroyed? What has lived on in spite of it?

Create a SoulCollage® card for this Hurricane and dialogue with it. Become aware of the wisdom and gifts it has for you.

Create a SoulCollage® card to honor the gifts you have received from this Hurricane.

If this Hurricane is too close to you and you can still feel the tumultuous winds on your emotional skin, give yourself some time, some perspective. Do a reading with your SoulCollage® deck where you ask, "How can I survive this storm with creativity and grace?" or "How can I see the possibilities in this devastation?"

SoulCollage® Example

Please visit KaleidoSoul.com/into-the-heart-hard-times
The password for this page is: journey

The topic to scroll down to is:
Katrina Trees
Note: The link to the slide show mentioned above is also on this page.

SoulCollage® Resource

Visit this page for more information about doing a card reading:
kaleidosoul.com/cardreadings

CHAPTER 66

The Lessons of the Bristlecone Pines

HAVE YOU HEARD about the amazing bristlecone pine trees* that grow only in isolated groves in the western United States? They are more than 5,000 years old and are thought to be the oldest living organisms known to humankind. They grow extremely slowly because of cold temperatures, rocky soil, and high winds.

Because of the high winds and rocky ground in their environment, it is impossible for rain to penetrate into their root system to offer nourishment and sustenance for growth.

But here's the thing. Insects dig into the earth and *feed off of the roots* of the bristlecone pines. This breaks off the tough skin of the trees' roots so that water from the rain can actually get through. Thus these amazing trees are *nourished through their wounds.*

And here's another thing. The bristlecone pines' trunks and branches are scarred by the rough winds. Then dirt is blown into the deep grooves, which makes the trees look beautifully tattooed. *They allow themselves to be written upon.*

What I take from this beautiful gift from Nature is that even in a difficult environment, even when chaos is blowing all around me and I am laid low to the cold, cold ground, I am still growing. I am still being nourished. There is always a way to open to nourishment, even if that means allowing my wounds to be the vessels for new growth and sustenance.

* I give thanks to Clarissa Pinkola Estes for telling the story of these trees in The Joyous Body, *an online class I attended in the spring of 2011, which is now available in CD format.*

Time for Reflection

In the journey of your life, what are some of the times when high winds and rocky soil threatened to stifle your soul's nourishment?

How did you survive the difficult terrain of that part of your life's journey?

What scars (visible and invisible) have you collected throughout your life thus far? Spend some time naming them and meditating on the particular beauty that they bring to your life. Is it time to make a card to honor these scars?

Do you have a SoulCollage® card for the part of you who is a survivor or thriver in spite of rocky, harsh life circumstances? If so, journal with it this week and see what this part of you has to say today. If not, decide if you'd like to honor this precious part of you with a card and start seeking images for it.

SoulCollage® Example

Please visit KaleidoSoul.com/into-the-heart-hard-times
The password for this page is: journey

The topic to scroll down to is:
Bristlecone Pines

CHAPTER 67

A Little Self-Pity Party

AFTER SEVERAL YEARS of decreasing vision due to a rare, genetic eye disorder, my husband Jeff was declared "legally blind" when he was 53. This diagnosis did not come as a shock; his eyesight had been steadily deteriorating for several years. However, actually hearing this diagnosis from a doctor did a number on our emotions, particularly fear.

Thankfully, Jeff's eye doctor helped to point us away from the fear. At one point he told us, "I want you to focus on what you *have*, not on what you *don't* have." He then proceeded to explain that Jeff was still far ahead on the scale of light versus complete darkness, that there was still a long way to go before he saw only darkness, if that ever does occur.

This helped Jeff immensely, and immediately turned his fears (and mine) into hope and a brighter outlook. It also made me stop and think. Perhaps this wouldn't be a bad mantra to use *every* day, even when the distress of such a diagnosis has mellowed into everyday reality:

Focus on what we have, not on what we don't have.

Right then and there, I seriously took a look at my life and made a list of what I didn't have, things I thought I wanted and had never received. I was amazed at how ludicrous it looked in light of the list of what I *do* have.

Once in a while now, I occasionally allow myself a brief "pity party." I am looking for some images to express this idea of feeling sorry for myself on a SoulCollage® card. My intention is to welcome and allow *all* of my feelings, including the one of self-pity. However, I find it better for my emotional well-being not to dwell on this feeling. Instead, I am learning to give it space, and after the space is given, to watch it fade. There is great freedom in the knowing that I can choose not to get stuck in it.

Most of the time, thanks to the wisdom and kindness of one particular doctor, I am focusing on what I *do* have, and the bounty of this flows into the rest of my life like one sweet generous wave of joy.

Time for Reflection

Make your own lists of what you Don't Have versus what you Do Have. Does either list inspire a SoulCollage® card?

Can you let go of continuing to grasp after any of the things on your *Don't Have* list and simply rest in the present moment of what you *Do Have?*

The next time you find yourself having a Pity Party, go ahead and allow it for an allotted amount of time. Half an hour is good. Set a timer. When the 30 minutes are up, let it go and start focusing again on what you do have.

Create a SoulCollage® card for the feeling of self-pity. Or create one for the part of you who is intent on focusing on what you have instead of what you don't have.

CHAPTER 68

How Many Clouds Does It Take . . .

A FEW YEARS ago my husband and I were fortunate to spend a week in Sedona, Arizona, USA. While we were there, we took a sunset tour of the Grand Canyon, an experience I highly recommend.

We left our hotel in the morning, climbed into the van with our experienced, happy tour guide (Stevie) and began the ascent into the mountains with ten other passengers. He took us through Flagstaff and we even stopped at an Indian Reservation for lunch. Later in the afternoon, as we wound our way around the magnificent mystery that is the Grand Canyon, I noticed a lot of clouds setting in. I also noticed my inner Worrywart starting to act up.

"It's getting really cloudy," I said to Stevie at dinner. "What about the sunset?" I was having sad visions of missing it altogether.

"Hey, the more clouds there are, the better the sunset is." He smiled wisely as he continued chomping on his steak.

I must say, I was a bit doubtful. I mean, it was really, *really* cloudy. But he was absolutely right. It was the most glorious sunset I'd ever seen.

So how many clouds *does* it take to make a beautiful sunset?

As many as Mother Earth provides on any particular day.

Time for Reflection

Are there any metaphorical "clouds" in your life right now? Doodle some clouds on a blank sheet of paper and name these clouds right now. Maybe it's an illness. Or a friendship that you need to let go of. Perhaps it's a lessening of faith, a temperamental teenager, or a difficult boss. Only you know what current clouds block the sunshine in your own life.

After you name these "clouds," remind yourself that light and color and beauty are present even though you might not be able to see or believe this right now.

Is a SoulCollage® card about Faith waiting to be created this month?

CHAPTER 69

Tears into Pearls

ONE DAY IN my teens I was working at our local library when a young woman came up to me. I was shelving books in the fiction area. She was in her mid-twenties and had an aura of sadness about her. I paused in my task and waited for the request. I wondered what she was looking for. A love story? A book about relationships?

Not at all. She asked for a book that would give her a good cry.

Well, no one had ever asked me for that before, but I was a voracious reader so I had some answers for her. *Dr. Zhivago. Love Story. Where the Red Fern Grows.* She thanked me and went on her way. I have no idea if any of these books helped her to "get her cry on," but this memory has always stayed with me. At first it was just an amusing anecdote to tell my friends. But then, as I grew into adulthood and life started "happening" to me, the woman's request became something else: a reminder that it's okay to cry. Even more than that, it's okay to *seek* tears.

I have shed many a tear throughout my life. When I feel sadness, grief, or loss of any kind, it is natural for me to cry. Heck, I have been known to cry when reading the newspaper or viewing a Hallmark commercial on television. Over the years, no matter what, I have learned that it is healing to cry. If I hold it in, then the sadness stays inside me and can actually do damage to my physical body.

Did you know that in ancient Roman times, mourners filled small glass vials or cups with tears and placed them in burial tombs as symbols of love and respect? Tear bottles, or lachrymatory, were also common in ancient Middle Eastern societies, and they are still produced today in that region.

In the Old Testament, there is a reference to collecting tears in a bottle. It appears in Psalm 56:8 when David prays to God, *Thou tellest my wanderings, put thou my tears in Thy bottle; are they not in Thy Book?* David is referring to the belief that God keeps a record of human suffering and always remembers our sorrows.

I have made a SoulCollage® card (see link below) to honor the part of me who isn't afraid to cry, who believes in the healing power of tears, and who savors the peaceful after-effects of a good, hard cry. Of course, when *I* cry, I don't look as pretty as the woman on my card!

All joking aside, this is a powerful card for me. In part, she says:

I Am the One Who cries and finds healing in my tears. I Am the One Who easily gives in to tears and doesn't worry about the judgments of others when I cry. I Am the One Who knows that if I cry enough, the tears turn into pearls. These pearls are gems of healing that bless my own life and others' lives too.

Time for Reflection

Gather images and make a SoulCollage® card to honor the part of you who cries. Or create a card to express the fact that God/Source/Spirit is compassionately aware of your sorrow, and has gathered your tears in a beautiful bottle for safekeeping.

Notice what feelings come up the next time your sadness moves you to tears. Are you simply feeling sorrow, or is your Inner Critic doing a number on you, causing you to also feel guilt or shame?

Remember that tears are always healing, and you have a right to cry, whenever you need to.

SoulCollage® Example

Please visit KaleidoSoul.com/into-the-heart-hard-times
The password for this page is: journey

The topic to scroll down to is:
Tears

CHAPTER 70

Leaning into the Curves

WHEN I FIRST met my husband, he took me for a ride on his motorcycle. I'd never been on one before and was secretly thrilled and terrified all at once. Before we took off, he told me two things. "Don't let go of my waist," and "Lean into the curves with me."

I nodded and straddled the black leather seat, wrapping my arms around him. It certainly sounded easy enough.

Well, holding onto him *was* easy. But leaning into the curves proved to be beyond my comprehension. He had to yell this instruction at me into the wind more than once.

It sounded easy, but I found it almost impossible to do. For one thing, as we'd head into a curve, my body's natural inclination was to lean the other way to bring us back to balance. I was frightened that if I leaned *into* the curve with him, we would tip over and wind up at the local E.R. or on the evening news.

Honestly, I don't know how we survived that ride, because he had to work twice as hard to maintain the balance of the motorcycle whenever I tried to bring about balance by leaning the other way! Of course, I can see now what he was trying to tell me, but at that time, my body simply did not want to let go of control.

That motorcycle ride was a big lesson for me in trust. I have since learned to trust my husband. Not blindly, of course, but when it comes to things that I know nothing about, I now know enough to trust his experience in the area and follow his direction. It was also a crucial lesson for me in letting go of control.

In 2011, life threw me a *lot* of curves: emergency doctor visits, biopsies, scary medical tests, surgeries, and more chemotherapy treatments.

During that curviest of "rides," I had to put into action the lessons from that motorcycle ride with Jeff so long ago. I had to trust the direction of my own inner leading *and* my medical team. I had to *lean into* the curves that life had thrown my way. Resisting a curve and trying to swerve the other way is only cause for more stress and will stop me from being able to embrace exactly where I am right now.

Time for Reflection

In what ways are you trying to control your own life and your journey?

Are you having trouble "leaning into the curves" that mark your journey's path?

The next time life throws a "curve" at you, see what happens if you pause, notice your resistance, and then breathe right into it instead.

Do you have a "Leaning into the Curves of Life" SoulCollage® card for your deck yet? If not, seek out images for one soon!

SoulCollage®:
The Big Picture

Overview

When reading through my essays as I organized this book, I discovered that some of them fit into more than one category while others fit none of them. I decided to group them here in this section because they all have something in common: they all speak to the "big picture" of SoulCollage®.

These stories describe how the suits are related, and how they are different from one another. They address how the SoulCollage® process affects our lives, how to deal with scary images, and various ways to enrich our lives with our cards and with the work that we do with our cards.

CHAPTER 71

The SoulCollage® Ocean

WHENEVER I LEAD an *Introduction to SoulCollage®* Workshop, participants are thrilled with their first card and eager to know more. When I was first starting out, I would try to explain all the wonders of SoulCollage® that awaited them, during that first class. As you can imagine, that got quite frustrating!

Let's face it, there is a *lot* that awaits us if we take SoulCollage® by the hand and allow it to lead us. There's journaling, getting to know our inner voices, learning about archetypes, doing readings, discovering animal guides, deepening our relationship with community . . . The list goes on!

Nowadays I tell excited newcomers that the process of SoulCollage® is like the ocean and what they have done by making their first card is merely to dip their big toe into the water. If you're still new to SoulCollage® you can probably identify with this. If you've been practicing it for a while, think back to that very first workshop you took, the first card you made. You got one toe wet . . . and then . . . you wanted more! So you took another class, made some more cards, found our Kindred Spirits community (see link below) online, learned how to dialog with your cards, made some more cards, did a reading, and so on.

You waded into the infinite waters of SoulCollage®. Some of you are still wading, on the ocean's edge. Some of you are now knee deep, and some are already swimming. Many of you have even set sail for deeper waters and are scuba diving, way down deep. You can choose to only skim the surface, or you can decide to dive down deep. Once you have been diving for a while, you can choose to skim the surface again if you want to. There are no rules. It's all about the exploration!

There are no limits to the gifts this SoulCollage® Ocean will give us, no limit to the depths we can explore within its reaches. If you think of it this way, you'll be more patient with yourself, and you'll give yourself all the time you need to explore. There is no need to rush.

Time for Reflection

Think about your journey with SoulCollage® up to now as a visit to the ocean. Where are you in relation to the "waters" of SoulCollage®? Write about this in your journal.

Give yourself permission to be where you are as you explore the SoulCollage® Ocean. Remember, it's not a contest; it's a journey.

SoulCollage® Resource

Visit this page for more information about our Kindred Spirits online SoulCollage® community:

kaleidosoul.com/members

CHAPTER 72

SoulCollage® Is a Mirror

THERE'S A WONDERFUL book by Suzanne Evans with the intriguing title *The Way You Do Anything is the Way You Do Everything*. This idea has always intrigued me. I once heard a yoga teacher relate it to how we practice the various postures. Now I am thinking of it in terms of my SoulCollage® practice.

At the end of my SoulCollage® workshops, I usually invite participants to share a few words about what they are taking with them from the experience. Usually they talk about how centered they feel after finding images and making cards, or how much fun it was to play like a child again with glue and scissors and colorful pictures.

There was one woman who responded differently to my question, and her comments made me look at SoulCollage® from a broader perspective. What she said went something like this: *Well, I've been sitting here for two hours and I've started three cards but I haven't finished any of them. I've been really enjoying looking through the magazines and ripping out pictures. I have all these nice little piles of images all over the table and yet I can't seem to decide which ones should go on which card. But you know what? I just realized something. This is exactly the same thing that is happening in my life right now. There's a lot going on, a lot of decisions I need to make and yet I can't seem to make any of those decisions. I'm hung up on gathering the facts and I'm kind of stuck in that place of having to decide but not wanting to decide.*

Everyone around the table identified with what she was saying. Not because they were also stuck making decisions in their lives but because they suddenly saw the process of SoulCollage® as a mirror that reflects valuable information about themselves.

Think about it for a moment. We all know that there is no "right way" to "do" SoulCollage®. The only way is *your* way and that might change over time. But look at how you've been approaching the process these last few weeks. Have you been diving right in and getting your hands dirty? Have you been avoiding it? By the way, *avoiding* something is very different from simply *choosing not to* do something.

Do you have stacks of images lined up but can't seem to get started laying out a card? Are you making cards intentionally but can't seem to make one intuitively (or vice versa)? Have you been making lots of cards but then putting them aside because you're not comfortable getting to know them more deeply?

There are a million scenarios of how you can approach this process. More than a million, I suppose. The important thing is to look at *your own* process at *this moment* in time and take note of what this is saying about other areas of your life. Not to *judge*, but simply to become more aware of what's going on inside of you.

Please remember the bit about *not judging* whatever you're observing about yourself as it is crucial to this process!

The woman at my workshop told me later that because she noticed what she was doing with the stacks of images, it freed her up somehow to actually make a few of the decisions that needed to be made. She never would have been aware of what she was doing if it hadn't been for her self-observations during SoulCollage®.

Time for Reflection

Take a look at how you've been approaching SoulCollage® in the last month or so. Look at any thoughts or feelings that are connected with what you've been doing and how you've been doing it. Remember, this isn't about judging yourself. Do not invite your Inner Critic into this space of observation.

You may become aware of another inner voice or two. You might notice any number of things! Simply pay attention to each awareness as it arises.

Journal or collage whatever you are discovering. *You don't have to change anything. The awareness is enough.*

CHAPTER 73

Intimacy – Me First!

IN THE LATE 80's I signed up to hear author and speaker Robert Subby who was giving a talk in Rhode Island. At that time in my life, I was trying to extricate myself from a quickly deteriorating, long-term relationship with an alcoholic, and was intrigued by the title of Subby's talk, which was *How to Have Healthy Intimate Relationships.*

I have to chuckle at myself now. I remember walking into the auditorium with my pen poised, ready to take notes. Eager and excited, I was going to write down every word he said because I truly wanted to know the secret to intimate relationships.

I left the auditorium more puzzled than satisfied, though, and my notebook was empty. Subby had spent the entire two hours talking about things like: taking care of ourselves, meditation, drawing boundaries, and being honest with ourselves about our feelings. I was really confused and disappointed, and a part of me was angry and wanted my money back. He definitely hadn't delivered what I was looking for.

Or had he?

Many years later, now married (thankfully *not* to the alcoholic), I came across the ticket stub from the lecture and was jolted into a major realization. Subby certainly *had* been talking about intimate relationships that night in Providence, but at the time I just didn't "get" it.

Now I can see and claim the wisdom that his lecture contained: you cannot have a solid, flourishing intimate relationship with someone else if you don't have one with yourself first.

To me, this is what SoulCollage® is all about - diving deeply and sweetly into relationship with ourselves. May we use this sacred process to know ourselves intimately, so that we can be in right relationship with others.

Time for Reflection

How's your relationship with yourself going this week? Has it been a while since you sorted through your saved images and made a SoulCollage® card to honor an inner voice, a guide, a family member, a friend, an archetype?

Is there someone in your life with whom you'd like to be more intimate? What can you do to deepen your intimacy with yourself this week so that you can deepen that other relationship as well?

CHAPTER 74

No Such Thing as a "Bad" Image

A WHILE BACK, someone in our SoulCollage® community emailed me this question:

Anne Marie, I am wondering if there is such a thing as a bad image. Last week I found an image in an old nursery rhyme book that is almost the exact image of how I feel about myself and my body/weight issues. But I just can't bring myself to create a SoulCollage® card with it. It's so ugly and heart-sickening. Shall I just throw it away and try to forget it or make a card and then hide it? It speaks no positive talk at all. It's like it's haunting me.

Perhaps the same thing has happened to you. I know it has happened to me! Don't we all have a couple of similar images stashed away at the bottom of our SoulCollage® drawers? Images that remind us of ourselves at our very worst? Images that haunt us with their ugly familiarity? Images that we wish had not found us? Images that won't go away no matter how much we ignore them?

With this in mind, here is how I responded to the above question:

First of all, I applaud you for cutting out the image and for saving it, even though it is nagging at you in an awful way. And I applaud you for listening to your own deep wisdom and keeping the image anyway, and for emailing me this question and letting someone else know what is going on with you.

If it were me, I would keep the image and not do anything with it yet. Do you have a folder or envelope or drawer . . . a place to put images that you've been drawn to, that you're saving for future cards? If so, add it to that pile, even place it at the bottom if you want to. You don't have to make a card with it right away. When the time is right, you will know, because you will find other images to go with that first image, and it will feel right to you.

Another suggestion. If it were me, I would look for an image or images that show the opposite of that first image. An image that might give vision to the way I'd like to feel in the future about my best self. I would seek out an image that portrays how I feel when I feel good about my body and my weight. Then I would make that card first. So when it's time to make the other, shadowed card, I could invite this brighter one to dialog with the shadowed one.

I applaud you for hanging on to the image. You were drawn to it for a reason, so it does have something valuable to say to you. It might even be a year or more before you find that you are ready to make a card with it. Just give it . . . and yourself . . . lots of time and space and compassion.

Five days later I heard from this woman again and here is what she told me: *The image has stopped scaring me already.*

Time for Reflection

Find a scary or haunting image in your stash of images, an image that you are drawn to but that you particularly dislike.

If it feels right, keep it out on your desk where you can see it often. Sometimes this alone will lessen its power over you.

Intentionally seek out images that represent the opposite of your "scary" image's energy. For example, if you have an image of a bloody bird locked away in a cage, look for images of birds flying free. If your scary image is of a woman plunging a knife into another woman (I actually have one like this!), find an image of a woman with her arms comforting another woman. And so on.

Create a card that represents the opposite of your "scary" image, and then dialogue with it. See if it's easier now to create a new card with the image that you don't like.

CHAPTER 75

The Sounds of SoulCollage®

A FEW YEARS ago I led a SoulCollage® Facilitator Training in Connecticut. On the final night of our Trainings, new Facilitators do a reading with their decks. They sit at tables in groups of four, and after I lead them through the first round, each group continues the reading at its own pace. Usually, after giving directions, I wander among the groups to see if anyone needs additional guidance or support.

In Trainings that I've led in the past, the tables were arranged in rows and I sat on a chair in the front of the room to hold sacred space for everyone as they were doing this deep inner work. At this particular Training, however, we had arranged the tables in a large square with lots of space in the middle. After I'd wandered among the groups and made sure everyone was okay, I moved my chair to the center of the square and sat down.

I truly love this hour of the Training weekend. Spirit is palpably present as people access their deepest intuition. Even though people are talking, there is a sacred hush in the room. Minds and hearts are opening all over the place! It is a beautiful thing to witness, to be immersed in, and I love holding the space for such deep inner work and community connections to evolve.

On this particular weekend I was given the gift of an added dimension to the experience. Because I was surrounded by card readers, I was being gently showered on all sides by the sounds of their readings.

Imagine it! From the front, each side, and behind me, I was hearing the beautiful voices of women speaking in hushed reverent tones:

I Am the One Who . . .
I give you . . .
The thing I want you to remember is . . .
I know that you can . . .

I want you to know that . . .
Your journey is . . .
My gift for you is . . . .

And so on.

I felt like I was in the middle of a sacred chapel and all I had to do to access divine grace was to close my eyes and listen, open my heart, and take it all in.

The sounds of SoulCollage® are all around you as well. Just listen, open, and receive!

Time for Reflection

Do a reading with your own SoulCollage® cards this week.

If you can, find a local group to do this with, or create one of your own.

SoulCollage® Resource

Visit this page for more information about doing a three-card reading: KaleidoSoul.com/cardreadings

Visit this page to find a SoulCollage® Facilitator Training near you: SoulCollage.com/facilitator-training

CHAPTER 76

SoulCollage® Lite

WHILE I LOVE nothing better than sitting down at my art table for hours on end to make SoulCollage® cards, I have noticed that sometimes I just don't have the time or energy to put into laying out images "just so," which involves using the frame, making sure everything "fits," and then gluing all the pieces together to fit on the mat board. However, not having time or energy doesn't mean that I don't have the desire to work with the many images that find their way to me.

I have quite a stash of pictures and it seems I am always finding more that speak to my soul! Sometimes I give myself permission to just glue down images in my art journal. Then I use colorful markers to write some *I Am the One Who . . .* statements on the opposite page. All of this takes very little time and yet I find it extremely satisfying. I encourage you to try it! It's a great way to keep your creative, imaginative muscles in flex, while at the same time keeping you closely in touch with your soul.

You might try this on a day when you only have ten minutes to spare, or you might try it when you're not feeling well and need to rest. For me, it takes away a lot of the pressure I put on myself when creating cards for my deck. I may call it "SoulCollage® Lite," but it brings me to the depths of my inner being, every time.

Time for Reflection

Try "SoulCollage® Lite" this week even if you have plenty of time to spare.

Go through the images in your own private stash and pull out a few that seem to be speaking to your soul today.

Glue one or more of them onto a blank white page of any kind of notebook, or just use a plain sheet of paper. Don't worry about placement.

Take a colored marker or plain pen/pencil (whatever makes you happy) and write some *I Am the One Who . . .* sentences from the image/images.

SoulCollage® Resource

Visit this page for more information about the *I Am the One Who . . .* exercise:

KaleidoSoul.com/soulcollage-cards-interpreting

CHAPTER 77

I Am the One Who . . .

THE BEST WAY to get into the heart of a SoulCollage® card is by letting the Neter speak for itself, beginning each sentence with *I Am the One Who* . . . But have you ever thought of using the *I Am the One Who* . . . exercise without a card in front of you?

If there is a pesky inner part of you who is getting in your way, you might not have time to actually make a card for it. However, don't let that stop you from working with it. You can give this shadowed part an image in your own mind (don't worry, you'll find the right magazine images later), and do some journaling from it even though you haven't made a card yet. Try it and see!

This also works with our brighter parts. For the last several months, I've found myself with a renewed passion for writing fiction just for the sheer fun and pleasure of making up stories. I haven't done this in years. Okay, I'll tell the truth - it's been decades. And because it's been decades, I find myself unsure how to go about this journey of writing fiction, or even what to write about.

I had never honored this part of me with a SoulCollage® card. But I can definitely imagine her in my mind's eye and I have already begun journaling with her, using the *I Am the One Who* . . . exercise. I have named her Alexandra, and she has much to say about what she wants to be writing, as well as when and how we might go about this new adventure.

There might be an archetype or animal companion that is calling you but you haven't found the "right" images yet for a card. You can still let this archetype or animal "speak" to you using the *I Am the One Who* . . . exercise.

There is also another way to use this powerful exercise. A few years ago on our KaleidoSoul Yahoo Group, Denyse shared an experience she had while stuck behind a slow driver who was going 30 mph on a busy street where the speed limit was 45 and there was no room for passing. She focused on the details of the car in front of her and noticed that there was an elderly gentleman in the passenger's seat. She imagined that there was a darling old lady driving, and began to do the *I Am the One Who . . .* exercise in her mind from that lady's point of view:

I Am One Who is a nervous driver and really does not want to be out here the morning after a winter storm. I Am the One Who is driving because I have to be out, otherwise I would be home in my bed snuggled up. I Am the One Who is keeping you from getting a speeding ticket or into a car accident. My gift to you is my advice to slow down and look around you. I am here to remind you that life is not to be rushed.

Denyse shared that this exercise helped to shift her whole perspective of an annoying experience into compassion and acceptance. She was glad that she chose to look at the situation differently, and it changed the whole course of her day.

Time for Reflection

Do the *I Am the One Who . . .* exercise with a part of you that you haven't made a card for yet. If you aren't familiar with this exercise, you'll find written directions at the link below.

Try doing this with an archetype or animal guide that you haven't made a SoulCollage® card for yet.

Practice *I Am The One Who . . .* with one of your Community Neters who isn't in your deck yet.

Try it from the perspective of your boss, lover, pet, or someone in your life who is causing you major annoyance right now.

SoulCollage® Resource

Visit this page for more information about the doing the *I Am the One Who . . .* exercise:

kaleidosoul.com/soulcollage-cards-interpreting

CHAPTER 78

The Changing of the Suits

I HAD BEEN practicing SoulCollage® for less than a year when something strange happened during a journaling exercise with my Joyful Transition card (see link below). This was one of the first cards I had created and when I first worked with it, it was definitely a part of my Committee Suit of inner voices, also known as personality parts. I knew this for certain because it was speaking to me as if it were *inside* of me, telling me a bit about what Seena calls my "local story," my personal history:

I Am the One Who is leaving something behind. I Am the One Who is excited about where I am going. I Am the One Who is all dressed up and celebrating this transition! I Am the One Who is moving into something new and exciting and different, and I Am the One Who can't wait to get there!

Yes, this Neter was definitely part of my Committee Suit, my "local story." I felt good about this knowing. I knew even then that we can't always know the suit (or even the meaning) of a card right away, but this one felt very clear.

Then one day, several months later, I drew my Joyful Transition card in a daily reading and when I journaled with it, it was speaking very differently to me. Listen:

I Am the One Who leads you to new places and people and adventures. I Am the One Who safely guides you through the open doorways to your future. I Am the One Who wants you to follow me wherever I lead you, even if sometimes that means leaving colorful worlds behind for black-and-white territory.

Can you sense the difference in the two voices? For me, it was like the energy on this card was now a *guide* of sorts. She was talking to me about the Larger Story of my life. I heard her telling me about many different transitions on my life's journey, not just the one I had been going through when I made the card. As I heard this, it occurred to me that this was now the voice of a Council card.

Then, of course, the part of me who likes things to be all wrapped up in neat little packages got very upset. "No, no, no!" she hollered. "That's not right. There's something wrong here. This was a Committee card. How can it all of a sudden be a Council card?"

It seems that I was still operating under the assumption that once I had a card labeled nice and neatly, it would be pigeon-holed forever as such.

I was so perplexed and distressed by this change of events within my deck, that I emailed my friend and sister-Facilitator, Karen Mann in Australia. She had been making and working with cards much longer than I had, and I really respected her wisdom about all things to do with SoulCollage®.

What a relief when she emailed me back, saying it was a normal occurrence for our cards to change suits now and then. She told me not to worry about it, to just go with the flow of it and to trust the process, to trust *myself*. She said that not everything in SoulCollage® could be clearly categorized.

How grateful am I for my Aussie friend? Pretty darned grateful!

It so happened that when I created the Joyful Transition card, I was right on the edge of a major life transition out of a customer service job I'd held and loved for 10 years and into a life of creating my own business. When I first dialogued with this Neter, it was telling me about that particular transition. But several months later, I was already "through the door" of that transition and immersed in the middle of life on the other side of it. When I dialogued with her at that point, she made the shift away from my local personal story (Committee Suit) and over to the larger story of my life (Council Suit).

This event stands out clearly in my mind now as a huge turning point in my SoulCollage® journey. After the "changing of the suits" by this one card, I was much better able to enjoy the mystery of the process and to let my expectations go completely.

Sometimes the cards don't just change suits; they change what they are "about." This is because *we* are continually changing and the landscapes of our lives are continually shifting. It follows easily that our Neters are also changing right along with us.

Time for Reflection

If you haven't thought much yet about the Committee or Council suits in your own deck, sort through your cards and see if you can better distinguish the difference.

Do the *I Am the One Who . . .* exercise with one of your cards that might be Committee (personal story) *or* Council (larger story). When you read it back to yourself, notice from which perspective it is speaking to you.

If you make a card about one thing and then do a reading with it later, it might tell you something else entirely. Don't panic! Just take a deep breath and trust the process. Trust *yourself.* That's all you need to know.

SoulCollage® Example

Please visit KaleidoSoul.com/into-the-heart-big-picture
The password for this page is: whole

The topic to scroll down to is:
Changing of the Suits

CHAPTER 79

Permission to Rest

I MADE MY Permission to Rest card (see link below) for my deck a little bit intuitively and a little bit intentionally. I had set out to honor the part of me who sometimes is lazy, and trust me, I wasn't thinking of this Neter in a particularly positive way. I had read about honoring our shadowed parts with cards and thought this would be a good place to start.

Imagine my surprise when, after I started journaling with this Neter, it told me: *I Am the One Who gives you permission to rest.* Of course, it said a whole lot of other things first, about lying around doing nothing, and not wanting to be productive for a while. As usually happens with this unique journaling process, sometimes after a lot of negative whining, a solid gold gift will pop right out! And there it was: *I give you permission to rest.*

Suddenly I was looking at this card very differently! I saw firsthand what Seena meant when she said that every Neter has a *positive intent and a negative potential.*

For me, this particular Neter's **negative potential** was the only thing that I had seen previously: the tendency to be lazy, to lie around doing nothing, all productivity stalled.

But oh . . . **the positive intent:** permission to rest. I could see the bright side of this Neter completely now. I could see its gift to me clearly.

I now call this card Permission to Rest instead of Laziness. I am amazed by how, when I was making it, I chose restful shades of gray instead of bright colors like most of my other cards. Somehow, I intuitively knew to do that.

Whenever I draw this card in a reading, it speaks to me about taking time away from the *do*-ing and spending more time with my *be*-ing.

I heard Deepak Chopra speak once about being careful not to suffer from "picnic deficiency." This is something I need to be reminded of on a regular basis, and I'm grateful for this restful reminder who lives in my deck.

Time for Reflection

Spend some time in your journal this week answering this question: *Am I suffering from "picnic deficiency?"* Seriously, when was the last time you stopped *do*-ing and just let yourself just *be*? Are you able to give yourself permission to rest even for just a few minutes today? Your body, mind and spirit will thank you.

Make your own "Permission to Rest" card and keep it in your deck as a reminder to give yourself a break from *do*-ing so you can enjoy simply *be*-ing. Remember that your card might look very different from mine!

SoulCollage® Example

Please visit KaleidoSoul.com/into-the-heart-big-picture
The password for this page is: whole

The topic to scroll down to is:
Permission to Rest

SoulCollage® Resource

Visit this page for more information about the *I Am the One Who . . .* exercise: kaleidosoul.com/soulcollage-cards-interpreting

What's the Difference?
Committee Suit and Council Suit

FIGURING OUT THE difference between the Committee Suit and the Council Suit seems to cause the most confusion among new SoulCollagers. This question *always* comes up whenever we are talking about the suits: *How do I know if this is a Committee card or a Council card?*

First of all, no one can answer this question but you! A Facilitator or friend won't be able to tell you the meaning of any of your cards or what suit they fit into. Not even Seena Frost would be able to tell you. This is because we make the cards for ourselves and only for ourselves, and we are the ones who know ourselves best.

In order for you to be more informed as to whether a certain card is Committee or Council, let's start with a visual description of what your Committee is and what your Council is.

Committee

The dictionary defines "committee" as *a person or group of persons elected or appointed to perform some service or function.* Chances are, at one time in your life, you've been part of a committee of some kind. A high school prom-planning committee. An education committee for your church. A committee to clean up graffiti on public buildings in your town. You name it; someone has probably invented a committee for it.

Think of the last committee you were on. Mostly likely, there were several people involved and each person probably had designated responsibilities in order to accomplish the larger purpose for which it was called together. Your inner Committee is very similar to the committee you were on. Within your personality are many parts that each have a certain role to play as well as designated responsibilities to carry out to ensure the Committee's larger purpose (which in this case happens to be your greater health and well-being).

Council

The dictionary defines "council" as *an assembly of persons summoned or convened for consultation, deliberation, or advice.* A city's form of government might be a Town Council. Certain kings were known to form Councils of wise men to advise them on certain matters. Churches sometimes have Councils that are convened to regulate matters of doctrine.

I like to think of my Council Neters as members of my own mystical Council of beings who have been chosen to advise and guide me. Sometimes I picture us sitting around a massive marble table, similar to the one that the Knights of the Round Table used. I also like to visualize them hanging out around a blazing fire in a wide forest clearing. When we meet together like this, I am not the "Chairman of the Committee," as I am when I am at my inner Committee conference table. *Something bigger than all of us is in charge whenever I am with my Council.*

Sometimes I meet with my Council members individually. I might specifically seek one of them out for direction and advice, or one of them might seek *me* out. Either way, there is a different energy at work than when I am meeting with my inner Committee members.

Your Committee represents parts of your inner world and your Council represents energies that are larger than you.

Time for Reflection

The very best way to discern the suit of any particular card is by listening to its voice. What is it saying and how is it speaking to you?

Go through your deck and pull out a card that *might* be Committee or *might* be Council.

Do the basic SoulCollage® journaling activity with this "mystery card." Then read it back to yourself out loud a couple of times. If the voice sounds like it's coming from *inside* of you, then it's probably a Committee card. If it sounds like it's coming from *outside* of you, from a voice that is larger than you are, then it's probably a Council card.

Even after this journaling, you might not have a clue as to the meaning of the card, or what suit it belongs to. You might spend a *long time* journaling with it and *still* not know. Remember that this is okay! Sometimes a card remains a mystery for years, so just be patient and keep it in your deck, trusting that it still has wisdom to give you even if it remains "unclassified" for now.

CHAPTER 81

How Committee and Council Cards Are Related

WHEN I FIRST started SoulCollaging in 2005, I was looking at my cards as separate from each other. A few years later, I was listening to Facilitator Karen Mann (Australia) speak during one of our monthly KaleidoSoul tele-classes. She said something in relation to the Council Suit that invited a major AHA moment for me:

> *The archetype is the overarching energy that you are attracted to. This energy shows up in your life in many different ways that give expression to your inner committee.*

My big AHA moment was that certain parts of my deck are related to each other! Here are examples of how Committee and Council Neters can be connected.

In my own life, Divine Mother has had a big archetypal influence on me since I was very young. Even though I have never given birth to physical children, this energy gives expression to my inner Committee via Neters such as: the Stepmother, the Cat Lover, the One Who Loves Children, the Grandmother, and the Aunt.

If the archetypal energy of Warrior is strong for you, it might actively influence and give expression to Committee parts such as the One Who Writes Letters to the Editor, the Political Activist, or the One Who Does Community Service.

Likewise, the Creator archetype will allow your Inner Artist, Writer, Chef, Decorator, Party Planner or Gardener to express themselves in various ways.

Time for Reflection

Spread all your cards out in one place and look at them carefully. Pull out any that seem like Council members (archetypes, spirit guides, or any Neter that has energy that is larger than you). Choose one Council card, and then choose any cards remaining that seem to be related to it in some way. Chances are they are parts of your inner Committee that give expression to this particular Council member.

If you don't have many cards in your deck, you can still do this in a more left-brained way with lists and words. Write down the name of an archetype that speaks to you and then make a list of Committee parts it might be related to.

CHAPTER 82

Stop Should-ing on Yourself!

A FRIEND OF mine recently mentioned that she felt like she should be creating some new SoulCollage® cards, as she hadn't made any in a few months. She wondered how to go about it, since she really didn't have any ideas for cards to make.

If you've been doing SoulCollage® for a while, you might feel the same way. Have you ever "shoulded" on yourself? *I should make a SoulCollage® card. I should finish the three cards that have been lying on my desk for months. I just made seven new cards and I should journal with them right away.*

Here's what I said to my friend, and here's what I say to you: stop shoulding on yourself!

SoulCollage® is just like any other creative practice: it's all about the process. Think of it this way: it's about the quality, not the quantity. It doesn't matter how many cards you made last week or how many cards you have in your deck. It's not a contest. There are no *shoulds*. There is only *allowing*. There is only *following the inner guidance* that is always available to you.

If you hear yourself saying *anything* regarding SoulCollage® that has the word "should" in it - STOP! Take a step back. Notice what part of you is saying this. Go to your journal and ask this part (even if you don't have a card for it yet) why it thinks you "should" be doing such-and-such. Have a conversation with it. It's likely that it needs something else from you. It's likely that you need to take a step back and listen more deeply to your IGS (Inner Guidance System).

Trust me, when the time is right for you to make another SoulCollage® card, you will know. You won't be able to stop it! In my own practice, it sometimes feels like the creative process of giving birth: seeds are planted (ideas for SoulCollage® cards) from something I read, or from seeing someone else's card, or just from an inner knowing. If I give these seeds time and a nurturing space in which to grow, then eventually they will "sprout." The right images will come to me and I will begin making a card (or cards!) quite naturally, without even thinking about it.

Our minds play little tricks on us all the time. These "shoulds" come from years and years of familial and social programming that might or might not be true. We don't have to buy into them; we don't have to believe them!

Time for Reflection

In what ways do you "should" on yourself? What happens when you add the pressure of "shoulds" to your daily life?

Think of a time in your life when you were able to stop and let go of your need to know something. What happened when you let go? How were you inwardly (and maybe outwardly) guided?

Find a way this week to take away just one "should" from your life. What happens? Journal about it.

Make a SoulCollage® card that expresses either the "should" or how you feel when you are free of it.

CHAPTER 83

Playing with a Full Deck

THERE'S AN OLD expression that I remember from my childhood. If someone wasn't acting "normal," people would say he "wasn't playing with a full deck."

Back then, the only "decks" I was aware of were playing cards. Early on, I learned how to play "Go Fish" and "Crazy Eights." I knew that a complete deck of playing cards had hearts, diamonds, spades and clubs, ranging all the way from Ace to King. Plus a couple of Jokers thrown in for good measure!

So the play on words was a good one. You couldn't really play a game of cards unless all the cards in all the suits were there. A full deck meant a balanced deck, a complete deck. If you weren't "playing with a full deck," then there was something missing; you were out of balance.

Now, stop and think. How balanced is your SoulCollage® deck? Are *you* playing with a full deck?

I would define a "full deck" of SoulCollage® cards as one that contains cards representing all four suits: Committee, Community, Companions, and Council. You can choose to call these suits by other names; that's perfectly fine. Seena says today that she wishes she had not named all of the suits beginning with the same letter as it can be confusing for beginners! So call the suits whatever you like, but in the name of balance and wholeness, do try to include some cards from each category.

To me, including all four of the suits in my deck makes it more whole and balanced. This is because each suit represents a different dimension of my own life. Committee cards portray the psychological dimension - my inner voices. Community cards represent the relational dimension - those people, places and pets whose energy has touched mine in powerful ways over the years. Companion Animal and Council (archetype) cards give image to the unseen energies and spirit guides who are invisible but nevertheless very real.

If I created a deck that only had Committee and Community cards, then my readings would not reflect wisdom from those mysterious unseen realms, the larger story of life. If I created a deck of only Council cards, then I would be missing out on the wisdom that my personal, local story can give to me.

The beauty of SoulCollage® is that it's so flexible. It's not like a deck of playing cards where you need 52 cards before you can play a real game. You can have as many or as few cards as you like. But do try to keep a reasonable balance to your deck by including cards from all four of the suits. Seena created the process this way for a reason, and that reason is wholeness and balance.

Time for Reflection

Take some time to sort through your deck. Even if you don't put backings on your cards to delineate the suits, look through them and determine if you are indeed playing with a "full deck."

As you look through your cards, make note of what areas are lacking. Maybe you have 50 Committee cards and only 1 Community card. Maybe you have cards for all your animal guides (Companions) and archetypes (Council) but not many for your inner voices (Committee) and loved ones (Community).

Set an intention to create some cards for your deck that will make it more balanced, so that you can proudly say, "I'm playing with a full deck."

CHAPTER 84

Cumulative Effect

I KNOW, I know . . . this sounds like the title of a *Big Bang Theory* episode. Just bear with me. I promise it's really all about SoulCollage®!

The dictionary defines "the cumulative effect" as *the state at which repeated administration of a medicine may produce effects that are more pronounced than those produced by the first dose.* For example, taking one dose of a cholesterol-lowering drug will not show an effect on your cholesterol levels, but if you take it consistently over a period of time, your "bad" cholesterol will be lowered and your "good" cholesterol will rise. If you have an infection, one antibiotic will not do the trick. You need to take every pill in the bottle for the infection to be healed.

I have noticed the same thing with my meditation practice. The first morning that I sat in silence for 20 minutes, not much happened. In fact, not much happens most mornings when I sit in silence for 20 minutes! But a month later? A year later? Now? I look back and see a tremendous difference. My quick temper is a lot calmer. I am more comfortable following my intuition. My inner voices are easier to hear and control. I take better care of myself.

And what about SoulCollage®? Sure, the first card I created made a huge difference in my life. After that, there were more cards, more journaling, more readings. Not a lot of noticeable changes along the way. But now? Ten years later? I look back and see the "cumulative effect" in powerful action.

Anne Marie Bennett

The results of practicing SoulCollage® consistently over a longer time span have been many for me:

- I'm now deeply in tune with my personal and creative rhythms.
- My intuition is *much* keener than it used to be.
- I am *much* more at home with myself.
- I'm more in touch with the healing power of community.
- My inner life is calmer and sweeter.
- I am learning deep compassion for myself.
- My self-talk is kinder and more loving.
- My relationship with the Divine has deepened and broadened in ways I never expected.

Did these signposts of self-growth show up in my life right away? No, they did not. When did they show up? I can't say exactly. I only know that committing to the practice of creating and journaling with SoulCollage® cards, and doing readings with my deck, has changed my life, both inner and outer, in vast and lovely ways that I never expected.

Did I notice these changes while they were happening? Not really. Did I expect these inner and outer changes when I began? I did not. The changes were infinitesimally small and unnoticeable along the way. Now here I am, looking back. I can see that those changes, like tiny grains of sand when added to other tiny grains of sand, created a whole new landscape.

Time for Reflection

Where are you on the SoulCollage® journey? Have you experienced the "cumulative effect" of this powerful process yet?

If you've been practicing SoulCollage® for a while, take a look back at your journey with making and reading your cards. What was your inner life like before you began? What is it like now? Take some time this week to ponder the cumulative effect that SoulCollage® has had on *you*.

If you're new to SoulCollage®, be aware that inner as well as surface changes *will be* happening, even though you might not notice them along the way. Trust in the process. Trust in the stories of those who've gone before you. Keep creating! Keep journaling! Keep digging deeper!

CHAPTER 85

Alaska Meets SoulCollage®

DURING THE SUMMER of 2014, my husband and I took an Alaskan cruise. The best part of the journey was when the ship slowly made its way through the Tracy Arm Fjord near Juneau. I experienced a deep stillness and immeasurable peace at the core of my being during this time. It was a four hour journey so I had a lot of time to just *be* in that stillness, breathing in the majesty of the wilderness that surrounded me. Yes, it was freezing cold, but the air was fresh and invigorating; it seemed to clear the cobwebs from my mind and body all at once.

About halfway through the fjord, I started thinking about Source. Spirit. The One who holds the Many. It was so easy to feel the presence of Source. I could feel Spirit running through my soul like warm winds and cool water all at once. I was smack dab in the middle of this Presence that holds us always.

Then . . . SoulEssence. Yes, of course. The spark of life that is within every living thing. I could feel that spark reverberating within me and was aware that this divine essence was also inside the abundant life energies that surrounded me on the ship, in the water, and on the heavily forested shoreline.

And Witness. The silence, the view, the experience, the Presence . . . all of this made accessing that nonjudgmental Witness energy so easy. I was there. All was well. It was as simple as that.

After those insights gently whispered upon the landscape of my soul, I started thinking about the four suits and what they represent. I wondered if I could sense how all of those Neters were represented there, in that time and place, for me.

Committee suit? Hmmm . . . I suddenly noticed that all my inner voices were *silenced.* Every last one of them! My mind was utterly quiet and still as we drifted down the emerald waters of the fjord. Something *larger* than my inner voices prevailed as awe and wonder took over my inner world.

Next I wondered what archetypal influences were at work here (Council suit). Looking around me, I asked and received many answers from the archetypes themselves: Mother Nature. Father Sky. Mother Earth. Beauty. Wilderness. Ancient Melodies.

As for Community, I was sharing this experience with someone I loved. I also felt deep connection to the others on our ship whom I could see standing on their own little balconies, and to our naturalist who was narrating our journey with many references to the mystical. In addition, I was experiencing a deep connection with the land, the water, and the sacredness of the place.

Last but not least, Animal Companions. Ah, yes! Who was present there for me? Bird. Eagle. Seal. Fish. I was also keenly aware of many other Animal energies beneath the water and wandering the mountains, even though my physical eyes could not see them.

I felt even more whole and centered after pondering these SoulCollage® components while standing in that sacred place. There is a deep beauty and an intentional wholeness in paying attention to the four suits and the Transpersonal energies *wherever* we are!

Here is another example of how this intentional wholeness can work:

Setting/Experience: I'm at a Josh Groban concert.

Source: I recognize that Josh's music connects me to the Divine so easily, so effortlessly. All I have to do is listen and Spirit is present for me. Why? I do not know, but I am grateful.

SoulEssence: I notice that my own SoulEssence responds deeply to music of any kind. I am more aware of my SoulEssence when I am immersed in song.

Witness: I can see the bigger picture of this evening somehow.

Committee: Some of my inner voices are brimming with delight right now: Inner Child, Sense of Humor, Permission to Rest, Music Lover, Romantic One.

Community: I feel connected to these other 12,000 souls who have gathered because we are all drawn to this artist's music.

Council: Musician is an archetype largely at play here. The stage is filled with singers, soloists, and an orchestra.

Companions: What comes to me is Lion and Lioness, my throat chakra Companions. They remind me of how much I love to sing. *"Open your own mouth and roar,"* Lion whispers to me as I begin to sing along with Josh and the audience.

Time for Reflection

Run the four suits and Transpersonal energies through your own mind the next time you are experiencing something powerful. Watch what happens!

Here's an additional challenge: run the four suits and Transpersonal energies through your own mind the next time you are experiencing something *difficult* or *challenging*. See if it brings you back to balance.

CHAPTER 86

Souls Colliding

FOR THE MOST part, I'm a happy iPhone user. The only thing that sometimes frustrates me is when autocorrect takes over. I have been teaching myself to slow down when texting or when using the voice function on my phone. Paying attention is also a good thing, especially before pressing the "send" button!

Recently I was voice dictating an email to a friend and I mentioned KaleidoSoul. When I read the email back before "sending," I noticed the loveliest thing. My autocorrect function had written "collide a soul" instead of KaleidoSoul! Of course, I changed it before sending the email to my friend, but those words touched a deep vein inside of me.

Colliding souls. Hmm . . . isn't that what our SoulCollage® community is? We are a glorious collection of individual souls who have bumped into each other on the journey. As our souls collide, we join our own fragments and pieces with everyone else's and a beautiful new pattern emerges.

Time for Reflection

If you have a smartphone, the next time autocorrect kicks in, pay attention. There just might be a lesson there for you!

CHAPTER 87

Write a Paper

IN MY JUNIOR year of college, heading towards a degree in Elementary Education, I stumbled into an Educational Psychology class that led me to the best professor I'd ever had. I'm sorry to say that I can't remember his name, but I'll tell you why he had such an impact on me.

His first assignment to us, besides designated reading in our text, was this: Write a paper.

Good students to a fault, we all looked at one another in puzzlement.

I raised my hand. "What do you want us to write about?" I asked, confused.

He smiled, then countered, "What do *you* want to write about?"

Someone else asked how many pages this paper should be. Our professor shrugged. "However many it takes you to explore the topic."

We got the same response, no matter what we asked. The only guideline he set was the due date.

I'm telling you, those three little words changed my whole outlook on education. Because the professor didn't tell us what to write about, I was free to explore what I was passionate about in regards to Educational Psychology. Because there was no word limit, I was permitted to write whatever I wanted. I chose the topic of Gifted Education, which I might not have explored if the topic had been chosen for us. Because of this, I found it to be even deeper than a passion, and I was able to lead a forward movement in Gifted Education in the small Virginia town where I taught after I graduated.

What does this have to do with SoulCollage®? Everything, dear ones, everything! SoulCollage® also gives us the freedom to explore

251

whatever we want to explore. There are no rules; there are no limits. The only right way, according to Seena Frost, is *your* way.

SoulCollage® meets each of us exactly where we are, and it proves to us time and again that we are perfectly okay, exactly as we are.

Time for Reflection
Make a card!

Acknowledgements

I AM MOST grateful to our beloved Founder, Seena Frost, who created the gift of SoulCollage®. I am fortunate to have met her, sat by her side, laughed with her, and learned from her gentle wisdom and humble presence. I am so grateful that she saw something special in me and invited me to become a Facilitator Trainer too!

Kylea Taylor, your encouragement, support and literary expertise mean the world to me. You have been an incredible role model for me during the last 11 years, and I have fully embraced the Protector archetype because of your wisdom and example.

I am grateful to Debra Zagaeski and Kimee Doherty, our ever-faithful KaleidoSoul Assistants. I could not do this work without you.

Anne Boedecker, I feel blessed to create our two KaleidoSoul SoulCollage® Weekend Retreats with you every year. Your wisdom, encouragement and artistic creativity touch the many who attend. You are a true Kindred Spirit, in every sense of the word!

Jeanne Marie Merkel, I feel blessed to have led so many SoulCollage® Facilitator Trainings with you over the years. Your joyful presence has touched everyone who has come to us to learn to become a Facilitator. You are a true Kindred Spirit, in every sense of the word.

John Pacheco, my big brother and good friend, it has been a pleasure and a joy to create weekend SoulCollage® retreats with you! I am grateful to you for pointing me in the right direction all those years ago. How blessed I am to have a Kindred Spirit in my family!

Thank you to Karen Regina, Kylea Taylor, and Jenny Perruzzi who spent many hours painstakingly reviewing this manuscript. This book is clearer and much easier to read because of you! Your encouragement and support as I worked through the creative process has been immeasurable and I cannot thank you enough.

Finally, my heart overflows with gratitude for each and every SoulCollager who has been a part of our KaleidoSoul Kindred Spirits membership over the past 10 years. Anne Shirley, the teenage heroine in one of my favorite childhood books, *Anne of Green Gables*, once said, "Kindred spirits are not so scarce as I used to think. It's splendid to find out there are so many of them in the world." I wholeheartedly agree. When I started Kindred Spirits in 2006, I felt alone with my SoulCollage® cards. Not so anymore! It has indeed been splendid to gather with all of you in virtual community over the last 10 years.

Resources

Want to learn more about SoulCollage®?
Visit these online sites for inspiration galore:

KaleidoSoul.com
SoulCollage.com

Become a KaleidoSoul Kindred Spirits Member and receive SoulCollage® inspiration 24/7.
Use coupon code NEWBOOK and save $5.00 for a full year.
KaleidoSoul.com/members

Take your SoulCollage® deck with you without lugging around your heavy cards. Use the iOS App at iTunes.

Interested in becoming a SoulCollage® Facilitator?
See current Trainings listed here:
SoulCollage.com/facilitator-training

If you liked this book, you will also enjoy:
Through the Eyes of SoulCollage®:
Reflections on Life Via the SoulCollage® Lens

87 More Thought-Provoking Essays That Explore
Life Lessons
Community Suit
Animal Companions Suit
Spirituality
Using Your SoulCollage® Cards
Available now on Amazon.com
For autographed copies and discounts on 10 or more copies:
KaleidoSoul.com/books

Private Facebook Group
If you'd like to share SoulCollage® cards you've made as a result of
reading this book, or chat with others who are reading it, please join
our private group online:
https://www.facebook.com/groups/1517960975185370/

Other Books by Anne Marie Bennett

Bright Side of the Road:
A Spiritual Journey Through Cancer

Sunflower Spirit:
26 Ways to Follow the Light
of Self, Others & Spirit
While Journeying with Cancer

Through the Eyes of SoulCollage®:
Reflections on Life Through the SoulCollage® Lens

All available on Amazon now!

CPSIA information can be obtained
at www.ICGtesting.com
Printed in the USA
LVOW10s0923010417

529285LV00011B/695/P